COOKING
POSSIBILITIES

Presented by
Nancy Smith &
Lynda Milligan

★★★★★
POSSIBILITIES®

…Publishers of DreamSpinners® patterns, I'll Teach
Myself® sewing products, and Possibilities® books…

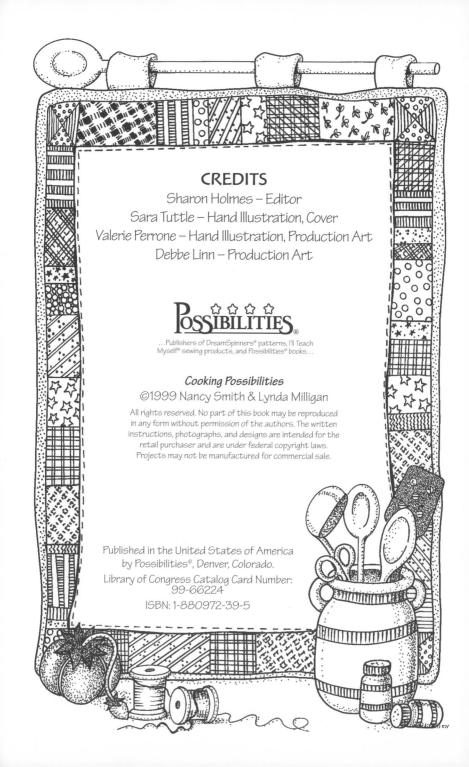

CREDITS

Sharon Holmes – Editor

Sara Tuttle – Hand Illustration, Cover

Valerie Perrone – Hand Illustration, Production Art

Debbe Linn – Production Art

POSSIBILITIES®

…Publishers of DreamSpinners® patterns, I'll Teach Myself® sewing products, and Possibilities® books…

Cooking Possibilities

©1999 Nancy Smith & Lynda Milligan

Published in the United States of America by Possibilities®, Denver, Colorado.

Library of Congress Catalog Card Number: 99-66224

ISBN: 1-880972-39-5

Dear Friends,

Great American Quilt Factory has periodic potlucks that everyone on the staff anticipates for weeks in advance. Crock pots bubble, the refrigerator overflows, and we have to bring in an extra table to hold all the tempting treats. The creativity of the wonderful ladies who work here isn't limited to their beautiful quilts—it extends into their kitchens and gardens as well. No potluck has gone by without hearing, "May I have the recipe?"

We decided to gather these recipes together and share them with all our friends. As the recipes came in, we thought about all the amazing potlucks that must be happening at other quilt shops across the country. We called quilting friends from various sections of the country and asked them to contribute. The result is delicious! We truly have a quilter's cookbook.

Don't worry, though! We remember what is really important—quilting! We've seasoned the book with quilting tips, small quilted projects for the kitchen, and information on five of the best quilt shops in the country. We welcome you to our potluck of recipes. Enjoy!

Nancy & Lynda, owners GAQF & Possibilities®

The recipes come from:

Country Peddler in St. Paul, Minnesota
Country Stitches in East Lansing, Michigan
Fabric Patch in Montclair, California
Little Quilts in Marietta, Georgia
Great American Quilt Factory in Denver, Colorado

MEASURING EQUIVALENTS

3 teaspoons	=	1 tablespoon		
2 tablespoons	=	⅛ cup	=	1 fluid ounce
4 tablespoons	=	¼ cup	=	2 fluid ounces
5⅓ tablespoons	=	⅓ cup		
8 tablespoons	=	½ cup	=	4 fluid ounces
12 tablespoons	=	¾ cup	=	6 fluid ounces
16 tablespoons	=	1 cup	=	8 fluid ounces
½ pint	=	1 cup	=	8 fluid ounces
1 pint	=	2 cups	=	16 fluid ounces
2 pints	=	1 quart	=	32 fluid ounces
2 quarts	=	½ gallon	=	64 fluid ounces
4 quarts	=	1 gallon	=	128 fluid ounces

 # FOOD EQUIVALENTS

1 square baking chocolate	=	1 ounce chocolate
1 cup chocolate chips	=	6 ounces chocolate chips
2¼ cups packed brown sugar	=	1 pound brown sugar
3½ cups unsifted powdered sugar	=	1 pound powdered sugar
2 cups granulated sugar	=	1 pound granulated sugar
4 cups all-purpose flour	=	1 pound all-purpose flour
1 cup shredded cheese	=	4 ounces cheese
3 cups sliced carrots	=	1 pound carrots
½ cup chopped celery	=	1 rib celery
½ cup chopped onion	=	1 medium onion
1 cup chopped green pepper	=	1 large pepper

BUTTER OR MARGARINE EQUIVALENTS

½ stick	=	¼ cup	=	4 tablespoons
1 stick	=	½ cup	=	8 tablespoons
2 sticks	=	1 cup	=	16 tablespoons

Great American Quilt Factory

8970 East Hampden Avenue, Denver, Colorado 80231
Phone: 303-740-6206 Fax: 303-220-7424
E-mail: info@greatamericanquilt.com
Web Address: www.greatamericanquilt.com

Great American Quilt Factory

Nancy Smith and Lynda Milligan shared a dream, and in 1981 began to make that dream come true by opening a quilt shop in southeast Denver. Their experiences as a social worker and a teacher, respectively, as well as their considerable creativity, love of sewing, and ability to surround themselves with talented people, have led to their continued success in the quilting industry. Soon after opening the shop, they branched out into publishing, first with a line of craft and quilting patterns called **DreamSpinners®** and then with **Possibilities®** books. They and their staff are currently working on their forty-eighth book.

Through their successful series of sewing books for children, **I'll Teach Myself®**, Nancy and Lynda have endeavored to teach sewing and quilting to the next generation. Pioneers in the photo memory quilt craze, they have published three books based on the techniques used to create these touching keepsakes.

Great American Quilt Factory has over 4000 bolts of cotton fabric, including the fabrics they design for Peter Pan® and VIP, hundreds of books and patterns, and all the latest notions as well as the tried-and-true. Shop services include machine quilting, photo transfers, mail order, and new-product information over the web. Be sure to visit Great American Quilt Factory when you're in the Denver area!

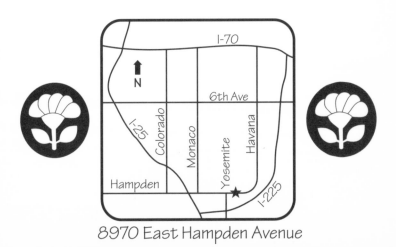

8970 East Hampden Avenue

PIZZA CRAB DIP

8 oz cream cheese, softened

1½ cups ketchup
2 tbsp horseradish

1-2 6-oz cans crab &/or shrimp, drained

1 cup green peppers, chopped

1 cup tomatoes, chopped

1 cup green onion, chopped

½ cup black olives, sliced

1 cup mozzarella cheese, grated

crackers

PREPARE – Spread cream cheese on small dinner plate or decorative 8" pie plate. Mix ketchup with horseradish and spread over cream cheese. Sprinkle with next 6 ingredients in order.
SERVE – Serve with crackers.

Judy Carpenter
Buyer, Show Coordinator

5

SOUTHWEST APPETIZER

16 oz cream cheese, softened
2 cups sharp cheddar cheese, softened

1 cup sour cream
2 oz taco seasoning mix (approx 1½ pkg)

3 eggs
4-oz can chopped green chiles

1 cup sour cream
1 cup picante sauce

corn chips

PREPARE – Beat cream cheese and cheddar until smooth. Add 1 cup sour cream and taco seasoning. Beat until fluffy. Add eggs, 1 at a time. Fold in green chilies. Pour into 10" spring-form pan.

BAKE – Bake at 350° for 35-40 minutes. Cool 10 minutes. Spread sour cream on top. Bake an additional 5 minutes. Cool.

SERVE – Leave in springform pan until ready to serve. Remove from pan and pour picante sauce on top. Serve with chips.

Terri Wiley
Staff

CRACKER SNACK MIX

2 6-oz boxes horn-
  shaped snack crackers
  or 10½-oz box crispy
  potato crackers
9 ½-oz box cheese
  flavored crackers
10-oz pkg oyster
  crackers
6-oz pkg tiny fish-
  shaped crackers

4 cups pretzel sticks
¾ cup butter-flavor
  popcorn oil
1-oz pkg ranch salad
  dressing mix
2 tsp dried dill weed
1 tsp lemon pepper
¼ tsp garlic powder

MIX – In a large roaster or large broiler pan, mix all ingredients well to make sure seasonings and oil are well distributed.
BAKE – Bake at 250° for 20 minutes, stirring every 5 minutes. Store in covered container.

Great to keep on hand during the holidays!

Jane Dumler
Designer

7

SPINACH CUPS

9 very thinly sliced pieces of whole
   wheat bread
vegetable cooking spray

10 oz frozen chopped spinach,
   thawed

2 tsp reduced-calorie margarine
½ cup finely chopped onion

½ cup light process cream cheese
   product, softened
2-oz jar diced pimiento, drained
1 small clove garlic, minced
1 tsp hot sauce
⅛ tsp salt
⅛ tsp pepper

CUPS – Trim crusts from bread. Flatten slices with a rolling pin. Cut into quarters and press into miniature muffin pans (1¾" cups) coated with cooking spray.

BAKE – Bake at 350° for 5-7 minutes or until lightly browned.

FILLING – Drain spinach and press between paper towels to remove excess moisture. Sauté onion in margarine 4-5 minutes or until tender. Stir in spinach. Heat thoroughly. Combine remaining ingredients in a medium bowl. Add spinach mixture, stirring well. Spoon mixture into bread cups, about 2 teaspoons per cup.

BAKE – Bake at 350° for 5 minutes or until thoroughly heated.

SERVINGS – 36 appetizers

One of my favorite appetizers!

Lynda Milligan
Owner

9

SWEET & SOUR BEANS

½ lb bacon, diced, browned, & drained
½ tsp dry mustard
½ cup cider or balsamic vinegar
2 large onions, chopped
1 tsp garlic powder
1 cup brown sugar

15-oz can baby green lima beans
15-oz can butter beans
15-oz can kidney beans
2 15-oz cans pork & beans

PREPARE – Simmer first 6 ingredients for 20 minutes. Drain cans of beans except pork and beans. Place all beans in 3-quart casserole and pour in the simmered ingredients. Mix gently.
BAKE – Bake at 350° for 1 hour.
SERVINGS – 12-15

This tasty bean recipe came from a family member in Seattle. It's an easy dish to make for a crowd, and it works equally well in a crock pot.

Jane Dumler
Designer

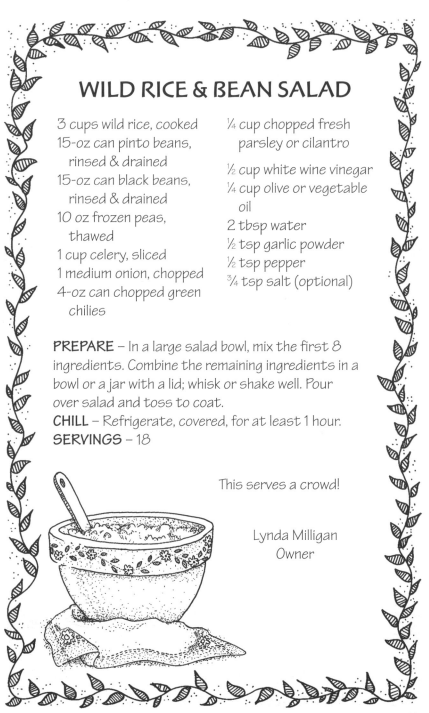

WILD RICE & BEAN SALAD

3 cups wild rice, cooked
15-oz can pinto beans, rinsed & drained
15-oz can black beans, rinsed & drained
10 oz frozen peas, thawed
1 cup celery, sliced
1 medium onion, chopped
4-oz can chopped green chilies

¼ cup chopped fresh parsley or cilantro

½ cup white wine vinegar
¼ cup olive or vegetable oil
2 tbsp water
½ tsp garlic powder
½ tsp pepper
¾ tsp salt (optional)

PREPARE – In a large salad bowl, mix the first 8 ingredients. Combine the remaining ingredients in a bowl or a jar with a lid; whisk or shake well. Pour over salad and toss to coat.
CHILL – Refrigerate, covered, for at least 1 hour.
SERVINGS – 18

This serves a crowd!

Lynda Milligan
Owner

PARTY POTATOES

11-12 large potatoes, peeled & diced

1 cup milk
1 cup sour cream
8 oz cream cheese
¼ cup grated onion

2 green peppers, diced
garlic salt
1¼ cups grated cheese (optional)

paprika or dried parsley

PREPARE – Cook potatoes in boiling water for 10 minutes. Drain. Mix next 7 ingredients and stir into drained potatoes. Place in buttered 9x13" baking pan or casserole. Sprinkle with paprika or dried parsley.
BAKE – Bake at 350° for 1 hour or until done.
SERVINGS – 12
TIP – Substitute frozen hash browns for the cooked potatoes.

Jane Dumler
Designer

MOMO GRIFFIN'S HEAVENLY ORANGE FLUFF

6 oz orange gelatin
1 cup boiling water
6-oz can frozen orange
  juice concentrate,
  undiluted
20-oz can crushed
  pineapple, undrained

2 11-oz cans mandarin
  oranges, drained

1 cup cold milk
3 oz instant lemon
  pudding mix
8 oz frozen whipped
  topping, thawed

PREPARE – Dissolve gelatin in boiling water. Add orange juice and stir. Add pineapple and oranges. Pour into 9 x 13" pan. Chill until set.

TOPPING – Beat milk and pudding mix until thickened. Fold whipped topping into pudding. Spread on top of gelatin.

From the friend of a friend of a friend in Tuscaloosa, Alabama. More fruit than gelatin. Heavenly!

Ann Petersen
Staff

13

CORN SALAD

16 oz frozen corn, blanched
1 cup chopped celery
½ cup green olives, sliced
½ cup green onion, sliced

½ - ¾ cup bottled Italian dressing

parsley
sliced olives

MIX – Mix first 5 ingredients. Refrigerate.
SERVE – Serve in a glass bowl garnished with parsley and sliced olives.

A recipe devised to satisfy a corn-crazy husband. Easy, quick, and lasts a long time in the refrigerator.

Jane Dumler
Designer

FRESH PEA SOUP

¾ cup onion,
  chopped
3 tbsp butter

4 cups fresh or
  frozen peas

3 cups water
1 bay leaf

salt & pepper
sour cream

SAUTÉ – Sauté onions in butter until tender and translucent. Add peas, water, and bay leaf. Simmer until peas are tender, about 5-8 minutes.
BLEND – Remove bay leaf. Put mixture in food processor or blender and process until smooth. Return to saucepan and heat through. Season to taste with salt and pepper.
SERVE – Serve with a dollop of sour cream.

Experimenting in the kitchen is one of my favorite pastimes. This recipe is a result.

Jan Albee
Wholesale
Manager

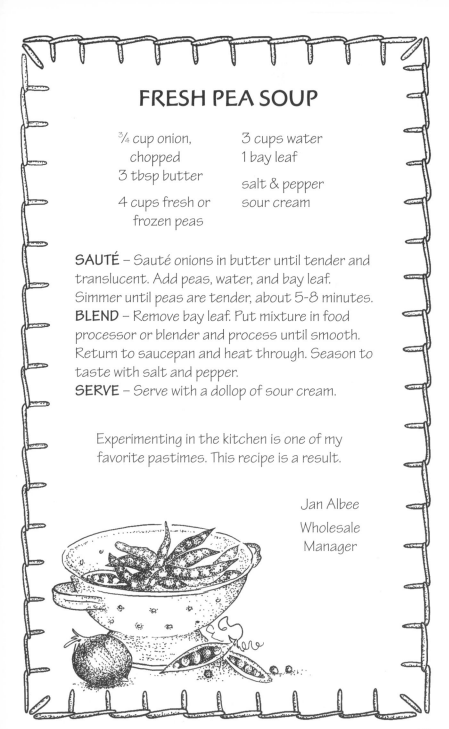

AUTUMN APPLE SALAD

20-oz can crushed pineapple

¼ cup sugar

3 oz lemon gelatin

8 oz cream cheese, softened

1 medium apple, peeled & chopped

½ cup pecans, chopped

½ cup celery, chopped

4 oz frozen whipped topping, thawed

COOK – Combine pineapple and sugar in large saucepan. Boil gently 3 minutes, stirring often. Add gelatin and stir until dissolved. Add cream cheese and stir until well combined. Remove from heat; cool.

CHILL – Cover and refrigerate for 1 hour. Fold in apple, pecans, and celery. Fold in whipped topping. Put in serving dish. Cover and chill several hours until firm.

SERVINGS – 9

Mom serves this during wheat harvest in Kansas.

Terri Wiley – Staff

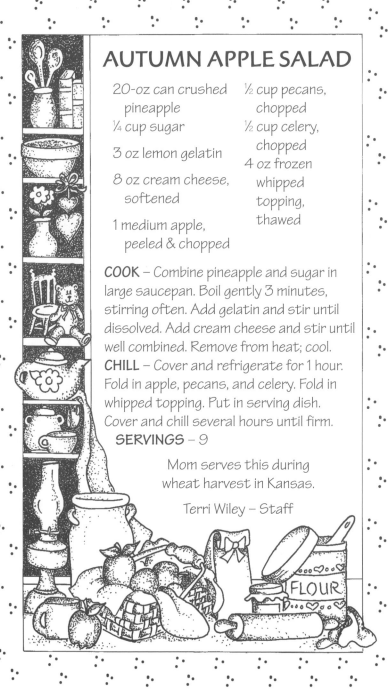

HOT CRANBERRY
CHICKEN SALAD

2 cups cooked
   chicken or turkey,
   cubed
1 cup cheddar
   cheese, shredded
1 cup dried sweet-
   ened cranberries
2 cups celery, thinly
   sliced

1 cup mayonnaise
2 tbsp lemon juice
1 tbsp onion,
   finely chopped

½ cup sliced
   almonds
2 cups plain
   croutons
salt to taste

SALAD – Combine chicken, ¾ cup
cheese, ¾ cup cranberries, and celery.
DRESSING – Mix mayonnaise, lemon
juice, and onion. Add to chicken mixture
with almonds and croutons, mixing well.
Add salt. Place in shallow, 7x12" baking
dish. Sprinkle top with remaining cheese
and cranberries.
BAKE – Bake, uncovered, at 350° for
30 minutes or until hot.
SERVINGS – 6

Judy Carpenter
Buyer, Show Coordinator

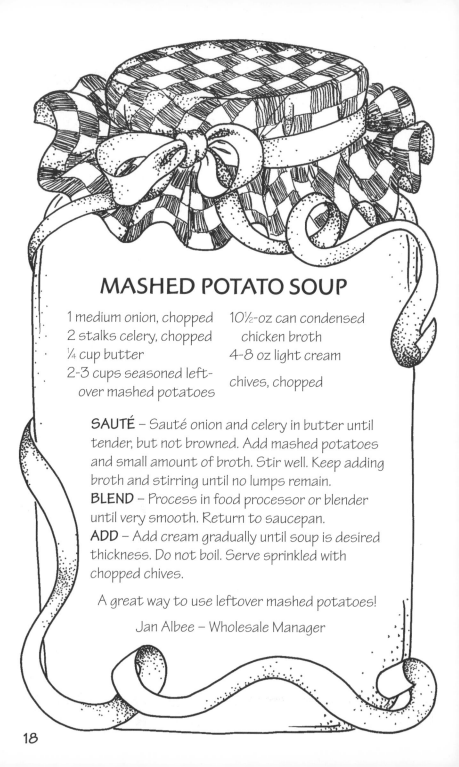

MASHED POTATO SOUP

1 medium onion, chopped
2 stalks celery, chopped
¼ cup butter
2-3 cups seasoned left-
over mashed potatoes

10½-oz can condensed
chicken broth
4-8 oz light cream

chives, chopped

SAUTÉ – Sauté onion and celery in butter until
tender, but not browned. Add mashed potatoes
and small amount of broth. Stir well. Keep adding
broth and stirring until no lumps remain.
BLEND – Process in food processor or blender
until very smooth. Return to saucepan.
ADD – Add cream gradually until soup is desired
thickness. Do not boil. Serve sprinkled with
chopped chives.

A great way to use leftover mashed potatoes!

Jan Albee – Wholesale Manager

ITALIAN BOW TIE SOUP

Sharon Holmes – Editor

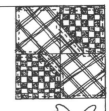

1 lb bulk Italian sausage
1 cup onion crescents
2 garlic cloves, minced

15-oz can tomatoes
2 10½-oz cans con-
  densed beef broth
2 cans water

2 zucchini, sliced
1 cup green pepper
  strips
1 tsp Italian seasoning
salt to taste

4-6 oz bow tie pasta
fresh Parmesan, grated

BROWN – Brown sausage and drain fat. Add onion and garlic. Sauté 5-10 minutes.
ADD – Add remaining ingredients except pasta and cheese. Simmer 20-30 minutes.
COOK – Cook pasta in a separate saucepan.
ADD – Add pasta to pot just before serving and heat. Sprinkle each serving generously with Parmesan. Serve with garlic toast.

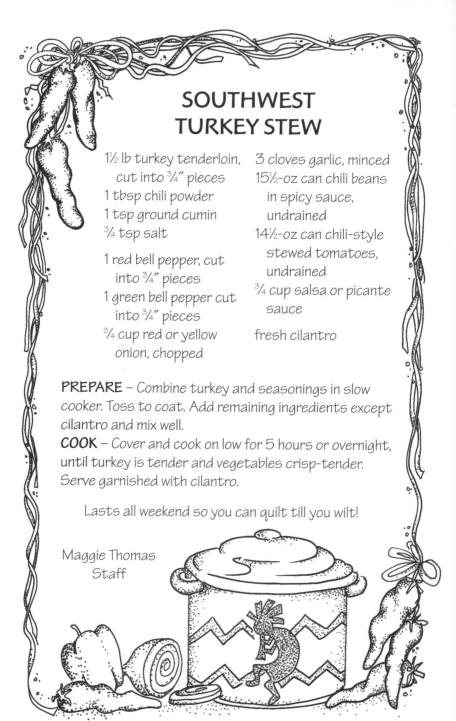

SOUTHWEST TURKEY STEW

1½ lb turkey tenderloin, cut into ¾" pieces
1 tbsp chili powder
1 tsp ground cumin
¾ tsp salt

1 red bell pepper, cut into ¾" pieces
1 green bell pepper cut into ¾" pieces
¾ cup red or yellow onion, chopped

3 cloves garlic, minced
15½-oz can chili beans in spicy sauce, undrained
14½-oz can chili-style stewed tomatoes, undrained
¾ cup salsa or picante sauce

fresh cilantro

PREPARE – Combine turkey and seasonings in slow cooker. Toss to coat. Add remaining ingredients except cilantro and mix well.

COOK – Cover and cook on low for 5 hours or overnight, until turkey is tender and vegetables crisp-tender. Serve garnished with cilantro.

Lasts all weekend so you can quilt till you wilt!

Maggie Thomas
Staff

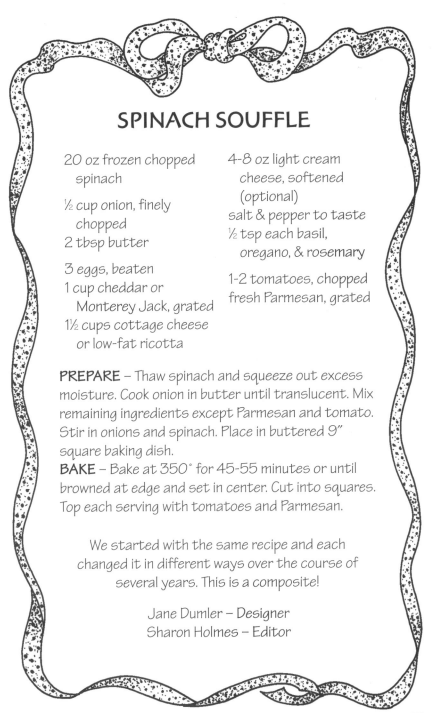

SPINACH SOUFFLE

20 oz frozen chopped spinach

½ cup onion, finely chopped
2 tbsp butter

3 eggs, beaten
1 cup cheddar or Monterey Jack, grated
1½ cups cottage cheese or low-fat ricotta

4-8 oz light cream cheese, softened (optional)
salt & pepper to taste
½ tsp each basil, oregano, & rosemary

1-2 tomatoes, chopped
fresh Parmesan, grated

PREPARE – Thaw spinach and squeeze out excess moisture. Cook onion in butter until translucent. Mix remaining ingredients except Parmesan and tomato. Stir in onions and spinach. Place in buttered 9" square baking dish.

BAKE – Bake at 350° for 45-55 minutes or until browned at edge and set in center. Cut into squares. Top each serving with tomatoes and Parmesan.

We started with the same recipe and each changed it in different ways over the course of several years. This is a composite!

Jane Dumler – Designer
Sharon Holmes – Editor

CHICKEN PASTA SALAD

16 oz spiral macaroni,
cooked & cooled
2 cups cooked
chicken, cubed
1 cup celery, chopped
⅓ cup onion, chopped
10 oz frozen petite
peas, defrosted

2 cups fat-free sour
cream
1 cup fat-free mayo
1 cup skim milk
1-oz pkg ranch salad
dressing mix
1 tbsp dill weed
½ tsp garlic salt

SALAD – Mix first 5 ingredients and chill.
DRESSING – Mix last 6 ingredients in a jar
with a tight-fitting lid. Shake to mix. Toss
with salad.

I gave this recipe to Nancy Smith and then
lost my copy. Now I can make it again!

Terri Wiley
Staff

CHICKEN TOSTADA SALAD

Dressing:
⅓ cup olive oil
¼ cup red wine vinegar
2 tsp Dijon mustard
1 garlic clove, minced
⅓ cup fresh cilantro, chopped
1 tsp ground cumin
⅛ tsp pepper

4 flour tortillas (7-8")

Salad:
2 cups cooked chicken, shredded
¼ cup red onion, chopped
8 oz black beans, drained & rinsed
7-oz can corn, drained
1 small tomato, chopped

4 cups lettuce, shredded
4 oz (1 cup) Monterey Jack, shredded

DRESSING – In jar with tight-fitting lid, combine dressing ingredients; shake well. Refrigerate.
SALAD – Bake tortillas at 375° for 7-10 minutes or until crisp and lightly browned. In large bowl, combine next five ingredients. Pour dressing over salad and toss to coat. Place 1 tortilla on each dinner plate. Arrange shredded lettuce on tortillas. Top with chicken mixture; sprinkle with cheese.

Goes together quickly. Great for warm weather!

Diana Leher – Staff

ENCHILADA CASSEROLE

1½ lb lean ground beef
1 small onion, chopped
1 garlic clove, minced

1½ cups picante sauce
10 oz frozen chopped
   spinach, thawed and
   squeezed dry
8 oz tomato sauce
2 medium tomatoes,
   seeded & chopped
1 large red bell pepper,
   diced

1 tbsp lime juice
1½ tsp salt

12 corn tortillas

1 cup dairy sour cream
¾ cup (3 oz) Monterey
   Jack, shredded
¾ cup (3 oz) cheddar,
   shredded

lettuce, shredded
½ cup ripe olives, sliced
additional picante sauce

BROWN – Brown meat with onion and garlic. Drain. Add next 7 ingredients and simmer 15 minutes.

ASSEMBLE – Arrange 6 tortillas on bottom and up sides of buttered 9 x 13" baking dish, overlapping as necessary. Top with half the meat mixture. Arrange remaining tortillas on top of meat. Spread sour cream on tortillas. Top with remaining meat mixture. Refrigerate up to 6 hours. If cold, let stand at room temperature 30 minutes before baking.

BAKE – Bake at 350° for 30 minutes or until hot and bubbly. Sprinkle with cheeses and let stand 10 minutes. Cut into squares. Garnish with lettuce, olives, and picante.

Make this early in the day and everyone will think you've been at home cooking all day instead of out fabric shopping!

Lynda Milligan – Owner

BAKED MEXICAN CHICKEN

4 eggs
4-5 tbsp bottled green chili salsa or taco sauce
¼ tsp salt

2 cups fine dry bread crumbs
2 tsp chili powder
2 tsp ground cumin
1½ tsp garlic salt
½ tsp ground oregano

3 large chicken breasts, skinned & boned

¼ cup butter

4-6 cups shredded iceberg lettuce
1 cup sour cream
6 tbsp green onion, thinly sliced
12-18 cherry tomatoes
1-2 limes, cut in wedges
sliced avocado

PREPARE – Beat first 3 ingredients. Set aside. Combine next 5 ingredients. Dip chicken pieces in egg mixture then in crumb mixture. Set aside. Place butter in shallow roasting pan in oven while it is preheating to 375°. Remove pan from oven and put in chicken pieces, turning to coat with butter.

BAKE – Bake, uncovered, about 35 minutes. To serve, place chicken on lettuce. Garnish with remaining ingredients.

This is absolutely delicious. I usually spice it up with hotter salsa.

Lynda Milligan – Owner

DAY-BEFORE CHICKEN MAC

4 cups cooked chicken
7 oz elbow macaroni, uncooked
2 cups cheddar cheese, grated
2 10¾-oz cans cream of mushroom soup
½ cup milk
1 small onion, minced
¼ cup green pepper, diced
2 oz pimento, chopped
4 hard-cooked eggs, chopped
5-oz can water chestnuts
1 tsp salt
dash pepper

PREPARE – Combine everything in large bowl and refrigerate overnight. Spoon into 9 x 13″ baking dish.
BAKE – Bake at 350° for 1¼ hours.

Another great recipe to make the day before, and you don't even have to cook the macaroni!

Ruth Haggbloom
Staff

ONE-STEP LASAGNA

1½ cups water
30 oz spaghetti sauce
16 oz lasagna noodles
15 oz ricotta cheese

8 oz mozzarella
  cheese, thinly sliced
½ cup Parmesan
  cheese, grated

PREPARE – Combine water and spaghetti sauce in bowl. Cover bottom of 9 x13" baking dish with ⅓ of the sauce. Arrange ⅓ of the uncooked noodles, slightly overlapping, on top of sauce. Spread ½ the ricotta and ½ the mozzarella over noodles. Sprinkle with 2 table-spoons Parmesan. Add another ⅓ of the sauce. Repeat with ⅓ of the noodles, the remaining ricotta and mozzarella, and 2 tablespoons Parmesan. Add the last ⅓ of the noodles. Pour remaining sauce over noodles, spreading evenly to cover edges. Sprinkle with remaining Parmesan. Cover tightly with heavy-duty foil.
BAKE – Bake at 350° for 1 hour or until knife goes easily through pasta. Let stand on rack, covered, for 10 minutes before cutting.

Now, this is easy! More time for the important stuff like quilting. You can add veggies or meat.

Judy
Carpenter
Buyer, Show
Coordinator

CHICKEN & DRESSING CASSEROLE

8 oz herb-seasoned
   stuffing mix
½ cup margarine, melted
1 cup water

2½ cups cooked chicken,
   diced
½ cup onions, chopped
¼ cup green onion,
   chopped
½ cup celery, chopped

½ cup mayonnaise
¾ tsp salt

2 eggs, slightly beaten
1½ cups milk

10¾-oz can cream of
   mushroom or cream of
   chicken soup

1 cup cheddar cheese,
   grated

PREPARE – Toss stuffing mix with butter, and water.
Put half of mixture in buttered 9x13" shallow baking
dish. Mix the next 6 ingredients and spread over
stuffing in pan. Top with remaining stuffing. Mix eggs
and milk, pour evenly over chicken and stuffing. Cover
with foil and refrigerate overnight. One hour before
you want to bake it, take it out of refrigerator and
spread cream of mushroom soup over top.

BAKE – Bake at 325°, uncovered, for 40 minutes.
Sprinkle grated cheese over top and return to oven
for 10 minutes. Freezes well.

SERVINGS – 8

A neighbor presented this dish to me hot
and steamy as I arrived home after giving
birth to my youngest daughter.

Nancy Smith – Owner

HAM LOAF

1 lb ham, ground
1 lb veal, ground
1 lb pork, ground
2 cups tomato juice

1 cup bread crumbs
2 eggs, beaten
salt & pepper to
 taste

MIX – Mix all ingredients and place in 5x9"
loaf pan.
BAKE – Bake at 375° for 1½ hours.

A recipe from my grandmother—a wonderful
German cook who had a great love of needlework.
She influenced me tremendously in my love of
quilting and gave me my first quilt.

Nancy Smith
Owner

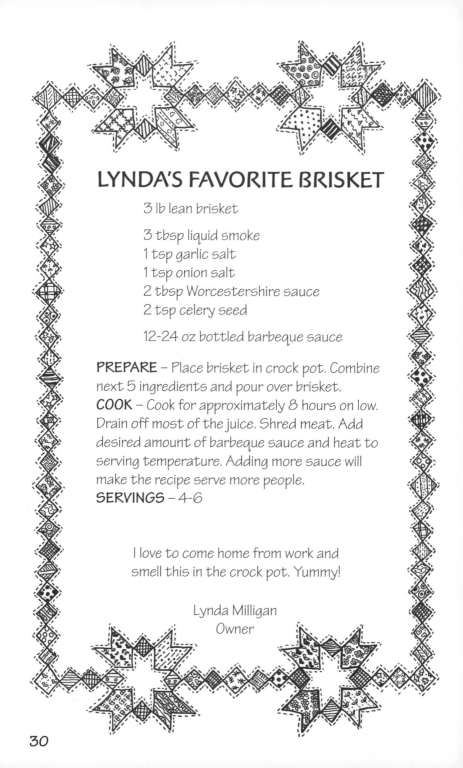

LYNDA'S FAVORITE BRISKET

3 lb lean brisket

3 tbsp liquid smoke
1 tsp garlic salt
1 tsp onion salt
2 tbsp Worcestershire sauce
2 tsp celery seed

12-24 oz bottled barbeque sauce

PREPARE – Place brisket in crock pot. Combine next 5 ingredients and pour over brisket.
COOK – Cook for approximately 8 hours on low. Drain off most of the juice. Shred meat. Add desired amount of barbeque sauce and heat to serving temperature. Adding more sauce will make the recipe serve more people.
SERVINGS – 4-6

I love to come home from work and smell this in the crock pot. Yummy!

Lynda Milligan
Owner

MACARONI & CHEESE PIE

My kids love macaroni and cheese. This version is almost as easy as the boxed kind but much more delicious.

Lynda Milligan – Owner

1¾ cups uncooked macaroni

⅓ cup butter, melted
1¼ lb sharp cheddar, grated

3 eggs, beaten
1¼ cups milk
1½ tsp salt
½ tsp pepper

paprika

PREPARE – Cook macaroni. Drain and return to pot. Stir in butter. Reserve a bit of cheese to sprinkle over top of pie and stir rest into macaroni. Mix eggs with milk, salt, and pepper. Add to macaroni and cook over medium heat 3-4 minutes. Pour into buttered 2-quart baking dish. Sprinkle with remaining cheese and paprika.
BAKE – Bake at 350° for 30-40 minutes.

31

BROCCOLI & CHEESE STUFFED SHELLS

½ cup mozzarella, shredded

½ cup ricotta

10 oz frozen chopped broccoli, thawed & well drained

2 tbsp green onion, chopped

¼ tsp pepper

12 jumbo pasta shells, cooked & drained

26 oz spaghetti sauce

additional green onion, chopped

PREPARE – In medium bowl, combine first 5 ingredients. Fill shells with mixture. Spread ½ cup spaghetti sauce evenly over bottom of 8" square baking dish. Arrange shells in a single layer over spaghetti sauce. Pour remaining spaghetti sauce over shells.

BAKE – Bake at 400° for 25 minutes or until hot and bubbling. Garnish with additional chopped green onion, if desired.

SERVINGS – 6

Very popular at our GAQF potlucks!

Jean Denton
Staff

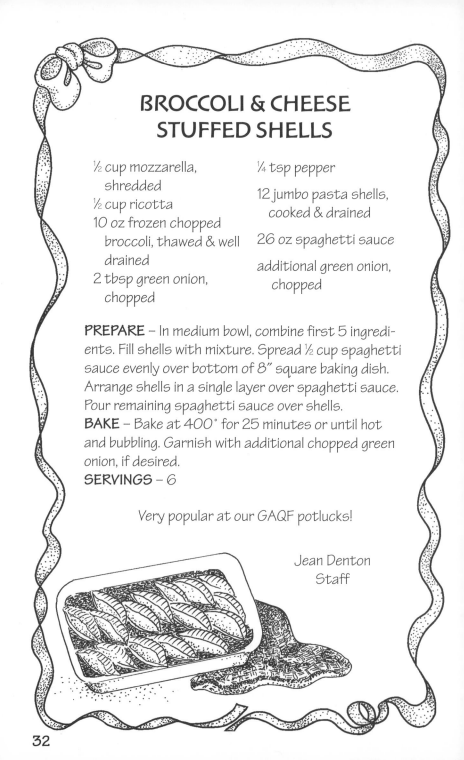

COCONUT BREAD

3 cups flour
½ tsp soda
½ tsp baking powder

4 eggs
2 cups sugar
1 cup oil

1 cup buttermilk

1 cup coconut
2 tsp coconut extract

Glaze:
1½ cups sugar
¾ cup water
3 tbsp butter
1 tsp coconut extract

MIX – Mix first three ingredients.
CREAM – Cream eggs, sugar, and oil.
MIX – Add dry ingredients to oil mixture alternately with buttermilk.
ADD – Add coconut and coconut extract. Butter four or five 3x5¾" loaf pans or two 4x8" loaf pans. Note: Placing a strip of waxed paper along bottom and ends of each pan makes it easier to remove bread. Pour batter into pans.
BAKE – Bake at 325°, 40 minutes for small pans, 55 minutes for large pans. While still hot, remove bread from pans and set on cookie sheet for glazing.
GLAZE – Place last 4 ingredients in saucepan. Boil 5 minutes. Poke a few holes in tops of loaves with a toothpick. Pour glaze over bread while both glaze and bread are still hot. Tip cookie sheet to spoon up extra glaze to put back on bread.

Sara Tuttle
Art Director

33

APRICOT COFFEE CAKE

1 yellow cake mix
3 tbsp flour
3 oz instant vanilla pudding mix
½ cup + 1 tbsp butter-flavored or
    other cooking oil
1 cup apricot nectar
4 eggs
1 tbsp butter flavoring (optional)

¼ cup sugar
2 tsp cinnamon
½ cup walnuts or pecans, finely
    chopped

Frosting:
1 cup powdered sugar
½ tsp vanilla
2 tbsp milk or apricot nectar

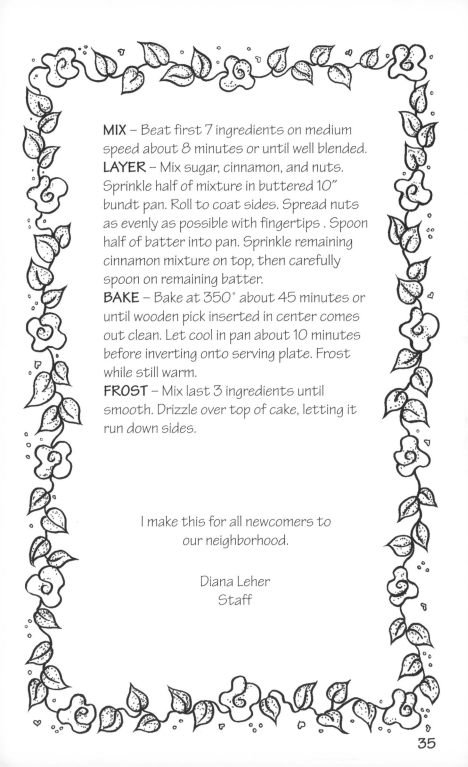

MIX – Beat first 7 ingredients on medium speed about 8 minutes or until well blended.

LAYER – Mix sugar, cinnamon, and nuts. Sprinkle half of mixture in buttered 10" bundt pan. Roll to coat sides. Spread nuts as evenly as possible with fingertips . Spoon half of batter into pan. Sprinkle remaining cinnamon mixture on top, then carefully spoon on remaining batter.

BAKE – Bake at 350° about 45 minutes or until wooden pick inserted in center comes out clean. Let cool in pan about 10 minutes before inverting onto serving plate. Frost while still warm.

FROST – Mix last 3 ingredients until smooth. Drizzle over top of cake, letting it run down sides.

I make this for all newcomers to our neighborhood.

Diana Leher
Staff

NOT-THE-USUAL FRUITCAKE

1 cup butter
2 cups powdered sugar
4 eggs

2 cups flour
¼ tsp baking powder

1½ tsp vanilla

6-8 oz pecan halves
1 lb candied cherries,
    washed in warm water
13½-oz box golden raisins,
    soaked in hot water 10
    minutes, drained

Jan Hagan
Staff

MIX – Cream butter and sugar 3 minutes. Beat eggs into mixture 1 at a time over 3 minutes. Whisk flour and baking powder. Blend flour mixture into creamed mixture at slow beater speed. Add vanilla. Mix in the pecans, cherries, and raisins, reserving 6 pecans and 6 cherries. Pour into 2 4½x8½" loaf pans. Decorate tops with reserved pecans and cherries.
BAKE – Bake at 300°-325° for 1½ hours.

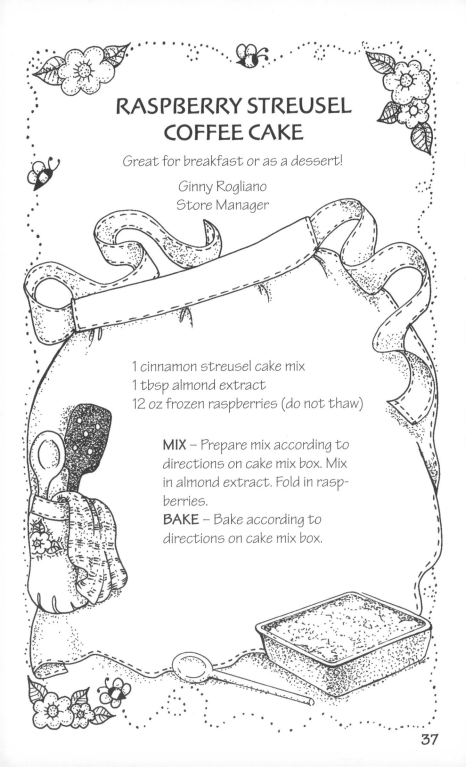

RASPBERRY STREUSEL COFFEE CAKE

Great for breakfast or as a dessert!

Ginny Rogliano
Store Manager

1 cinnamon streusel cake mix
1 tbsp almond extract
12 oz frozen raspberries (do not thaw)

MIX – Prepare mix according to directions on cake mix box. Mix in almond extract. Fold in raspberries.
BAKE – Bake according to directions on cake mix box.

SOUR CREAM APPLE PIE

1 cup sour cream
1 large egg, lightly beaten
2 teaspoons vanilla
¾ cup sugar
⅛ tsp salt
¼ cup all-purpose flour

2 lb Granny Smith apples, peeled, cored, & thinly sliced

9" deep-dish pastry shell, unbaked

⅓ cup all-purpose flour
¼ cup sugar
¼ cup light brown sugar, packed
2½ tsp ground cinnamon
¾ cup walnuts, chopped
6 tbsp unsalted butter, chilled, cut into pieces

FILLING – Combine first 6 ingredients, stirring until well blended. Stir in apples. Pour into pastry shell.
BAKE – Bake at 425° for 10 minutes. Reduce heat to 350° and bake an additional 30 minutes.
TOPPING – Combine last 6 ingredients, blending until mixture resembles coarse meal. Spoon topping over pie.
BAKE – Bake at 350° for 15-20 minutes or until filling is bubbly.

The recipe I use for my best friend's birthday cake every year!

Ginny Rogliano
Store Manager

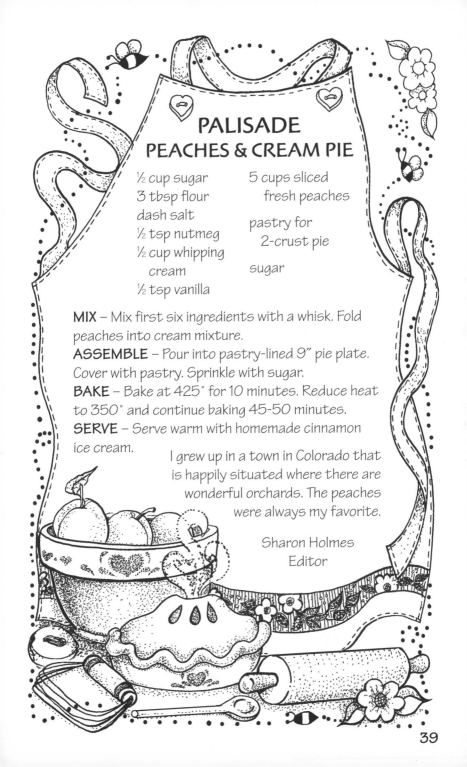

PALISADE
PEACHES & CREAM PIE

½ cup sugar
3 tbsp flour
dash salt
½ tsp nutmeg
½ cup whipping
cream
½ tsp vanilla

5 cups sliced
fresh peaches

pastry for
2-crust pie

sugar

MIX – Mix first six ingredients with a whisk. Fold peaches into cream mixture.
ASSEMBLE – Pour into pastry-lined 9" pie plate. Cover with pastry. Sprinkle with sugar.
BAKE – Bake at 425° for 10 minutes. Reduce heat to 350° and continue baking 45-50 minutes.
SERVE – Serve warm with homemade cinnamon ice cream.

I grew up in a town in Colorado that is happily situated where there are wonderful orchards. The peaches were always my favorite.

Sharon Holmes
Editor

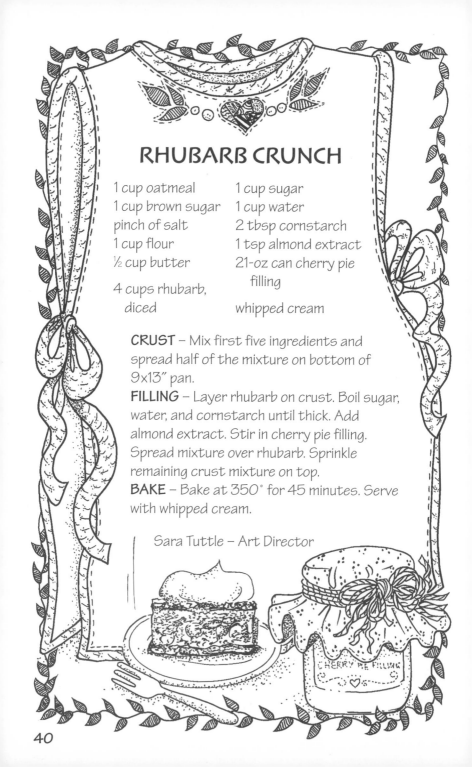

RHUBARB CRUNCH

1 cup oatmeal
1 cup brown sugar
pinch of salt
1 cup flour
½ cup butter

4 cups rhubarb,
  diced

1 cup sugar
1 cup water
2 tbsp cornstarch
1 tsp almond extract
21-oz can cherry pie
  filling

whipped cream

CRUST – Mix first five ingredients and spread half of the mixture on bottom of 9x13" pan.

FILLING – Layer rhubarb on crust. Boil sugar, water, and cornstarch until thick. Add almond extract. Stir in cherry pie filling. Spread mixture over rhubarb. Sprinkle remaining crust mixture on top.

BAKE – Bake at 350° for 45 minutes. Serve with whipped cream.

Sara Tuttle – Art Director

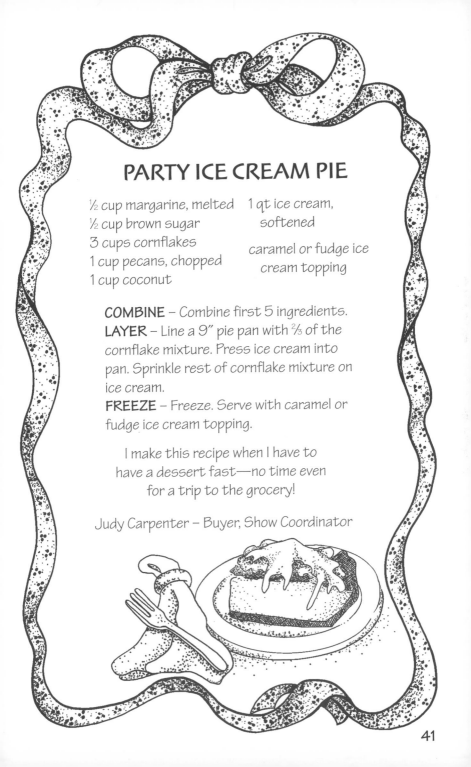

PARTY ICE CREAM PIE

½ cup margarine, melted
½ cup brown sugar
3 cups cornflakes
1 cup pecans, chopped
1 cup coconut

1 qt ice cream, softened

caramel or fudge ice cream topping

COMBINE – Combine first 5 ingredients.
LAYER – Line a 9" pie pan with ⅔ of the cornflake mixture. Press ice cream into pan. Sprinkle rest of cornflake mixture on ice cream.
FREEZE – Freeze. Serve with caramel or fudge ice cream topping.

I make this recipe when I have to have a dessert fast—no time even for a trip to the grocery!

Judy Carpenter – Buyer, Show Coordinator

PINEAPPLE PIE

¾ cup sugar
¼ cup flour
½ tsp salt

15¼-oz can crushed
   pineapple
1 cup sour cream
1 tbsp lemon juice

2 egg yolks, slightly beaten

9″ baked pie crust

4 egg whites
¼ tsp cream of tarter
½ cup sugar
½ tsp vanilla

COOK – Combine sugar, flour, and salt in saucepan. Stir in pineapple, sour cream and lemon juice. Cook, stirring constantly until mixture comes to a boil and thickens. Cook 2 minutes longer. Stir a small amount of hot mixture into egg yolks then pour back into pan, stirring constantly. Cook 2 minutes longer.

COOL – Cool at room temperature. Spoon into pie shell.

MERINGUE – Beat egg whites and cream of tarter until frothy. Add vanilla. Add sugar gradually while beating until stiff. Top pie with meringue and bake at 350° for 12-15 minutes or until slightly browned.

I was given this recipe by a fellow military wife about 30 years ago and have been making it ever since. Yummy!

Jan Hagan – Staff

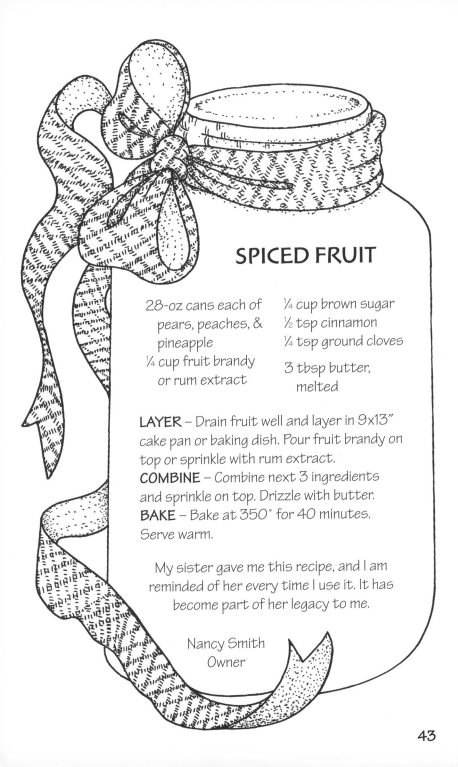

SPICED FRUIT

28-oz cans each of
pears, peaches, &
pineapple
¼ cup fruit brandy
or rum extract

¼ cup brown sugar
½ tsp cinnamon
¼ tsp ground cloves

3 tbsp butter,
melted

LAYER – Drain fruit well and layer in 9x13"
cake pan or baking dish. Pour fruit brandy on
top or sprinkle with rum extract.
COMBINE – Combine next 3 ingredients
and sprinkle on top. Drizzle with butter.
BAKE – Bake at 350° for 40 minutes.
Serve warm.

My sister gave me this recipe, and I am
reminded of her every time I use it. It has
become part of her legacy to me.

Nancy Smith
Owner

QUILTING HINTS

Use a white terry bath towel on the ironing board for pressing applique, embroidery, and even patchwork. Applique and embroidery designs will sink into the nap of the terry cloth and give a nice raised effect to the work. Collecting loose fibers, protecting the ironing board cover, and easy washing are its other high points.

Cut a piece of Molefoam® to place on the sewing machine as a ¼" seam guide.

Use table salt for removing remnants of fusible web from your iron. Put the salt on a non-stick applique ironing sheet or wax paper and iron over it.

Wet your finger and run it down the back of your sewing machine needle to make threading the needle easier.

Take ballpoint pen ink out of fabric by spraying with hairspray and then washing normally.

Your rotary blade may not be as dull as you think. Carefully clean the edge of it with sewing machine oil on a paper towel.

The Country Peddler Quilt Shop

2230 Carter Avenue, St. Paul, Minnesota 55108
Phone: 651-646-1756 Fax: 651-645-6899
E-mail: quilts@countrypeddler.com
Web Address: www.countrypeddler.com

The Country Peddler Quilt Shop

The Country Peddler started in 1972 with twelve bolts of fabric. Over the years the fabric stock has grown to 6000 bolts. This large inventory is beautifully spread among the small rooms of a charming turn-of-the-century structure in Milton Square in St. Paul, Minnesota.

Owned by Jean Humenansky, with her mother Jeanette Michel, The Country Peddler has a commitment to the community. The shop participates in food drives, fabric and quilt donations, and guild sponsorship.

Country Peddler offers a wonderful selection of contemporary batiks and homespuns, a year-round inventory of Christmas fabrics, and has a little of everything in between. The shop is well known for its two floors of samples and ideas. The staff makes you feel at home in the friendly atmosphere while you browse through baskets and bins of fabric bundles and kits selected especially for busy quilters. More inspiration can be found in the hundreds of patterns and books, the latest notions, and more.

The Country Peddler is located midway between St. Paul and Minneapolis, is twenty minutes from the Mall of America, and is open seven days a week. Chosen as a 1997 Top Ten Quilt Shop by American Quilting and Patchwork Magazine, this is definitely a quilt shop not to be missed.

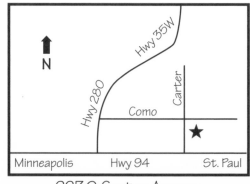

2230 Carter Avenue

PARMESAN & ARTICHOKE DIP

½ cup green onions, finely
  chopped
14-oz can artichoke
  hearts, drained & diced
1 cup mayonnaise

1 cup fresh Parmesan
  cheese, grated
dash garlic powder
dash Beau Monde
  seasoning

PREPARE – Combine all ingredients. Spoon into 1-quart casserole.

BAKE – Bake at 350° until bubbly, about 20 minutes.

SERVE – Serve with crackers, bread rounds, or vegetables.

MAKES – 2½ cups

This
piping hot cocktail
spread will have them requesting
the recipe after one bite.

Ann Palmer
Staff

WILD RICE SOUP

1 tbsp minced onion
2 tbsp butter

¼ cup flour
4 cups chicken broth

½ tsp salt
2 cups cooked wild rice
1 cup light cream

minced parsley
⅓ cup ham, minced
⅓ cup carrot, finely
   grated
3 tbsp slivered
   almonds

PREPARE – Sauté onion in butter. Stir in flour. Slowly add chicken broth, stirring so the mixture stays smooth. Bring to a boil and then simmer 5 minutes.

ADD – Add salt, rice, and cream. Heat to serving temperature. Add parsley, ham, carrot, and almonds.

I use this soup to lure my quilting buddies over to help me baste my quilts.

Peggy Hildebrand
Staff, Quilting Teacher

THE BEST BRAN MUFFINS

5 cups bran cereal
1½ cups unprocessed bran
4 cups buttermilk, room temperature

6 large eggs, room temp
¾ cup butter, melted, cooled
½ cup vegetable oil
½ cup molasses
1 tsp vanilla extract

1 cup packed brown sugar

5½ cups all-purpose flour
1 tbsp baking powder
2 tsp baking soda
1½ tsp salt

PREPARE – Combine bran cereal and bran. Stir in buttermilk and let stand until absorbed. In another bowl, combine eggs, butter, oil, molasses, and vanilla. Stir in brown sugar and then bran mixture. In a very large bowl, combine remaining ingredients. Make a well in the center and add liquid mixture. Stir just to combine. Optional: Chill for up to two weeks.

BAKE – Lightly butter muffin cups. Fill each with ⅓ cup batter and bake at 400° for 17-22 minutes. Increase baking time by 5 minutes if batter is chilled. Cool 5 minutes before removing from pan. Makes approximately 32 muffins. These muffins freeze well.

TIP – Fill unused cups half full of water to avoid warping the pan.

Dee Dee Liebrecht – Staff

BEST-EVER RASPBERRY SALAD

2 cups boiling water
6 oz raspberry gelatin
1½ cups applesauce
20 oz frozen raspberries

½ of 10-oz bag miniature
   marshmallows
2 cups sour cream

SALAD – Dissolve gelatin in boiling water. Chill until partially set. Add applesauce and berries. Chill until set.

OPTIONAL DRESSING – Blend marshmallows and sour cream well. Serve with salad.

Laurie Toensing
Staff, Teacher, Machine Quilter

ORIENTAL CHICKEN SALAD

2 seasoning packets
  from ramen
  noodles
2 tbsp sugar
1 cup salad oil
1 tsp salt
1 tsp pepper
6 tbsp rice vinegar

3 oz slivered
  almonds

4-5 chicken breasts,
  cooked & cubed

6-8 cups cabbage,
  shredded
1 small onion, diced
4 tbsp sunflower
  seeds
2 pkg ramen noodles,
  broken

DRESSING – Blend first 6 ingredients and chill overnight.

TOAST – Toast almonds at 350° for 10 minutes.

MIX – Mix chicken and almonds with remaining four salad ingredients.

TOSS – Toss dressing with salad and serve.

Melanie Humenansky
Daughter-in-Law of Owner

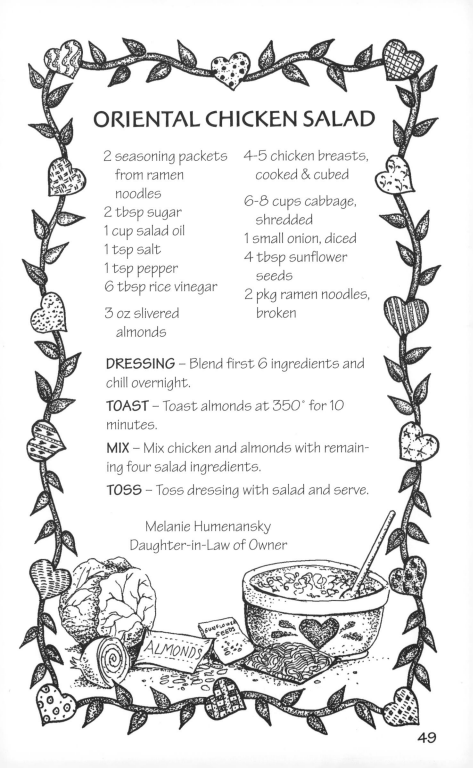

GREEK VEGETABLES

3-4 zucchini	¼ cup olive oil
4-5 potatoes	14½-oz can stewed
2 fresh tomatoes	tomatoes
1 onion	2 tbsp fresh dill
2 cups fresh green	2 tbsp fresh parsley
beans	salt & pepper to taste

PREPARE – Cut vegetables into large slices. Place in 10x15" baking pan. Toss with oil, stewed tomatoes, and seasonings.

BAKE – Bake at 400° for 30 minutes. Lower heat to 325° and continue to bake for 1½ hours, stirring occasionally. Cover loosely with foil, if necessary, to prevent drying.

Every summer for the last seven years, Jan and Carol from Hearthside Quilter's Nook in Milwaukee, Mimi from SPPS Publishing in Las Vegas, and I get together to sew and swim at "the lake" in Wisconsin. Quick and easy recipes are fixed to get the maximum sew time! Greek Vegetables has been a favorite of ours.

Jean Humenansky
Owner

ITALIAN DIP SANDWICHES

3-4 lb beef arm or pot roast
1 large onion, sliced into crescents
8 oz fat-free Italian salad dressing

large deli-style sandwich rolls

PREPARE – Place roast in crock pot. Add sliced onion and dressing. Cover.

COOK – Cook at low heat for at least 8 hours. Just before serving, pull beef apart with two forks. Serve on rolls with cooking liquid on the side for dipping.

This is a great meal to start early in the day so you can quilt without interruption. Warning: The smell will drive you crazy all day long!

Helen Thorn
PineTree Lodge Designs,
Machine Quilting
Teacher

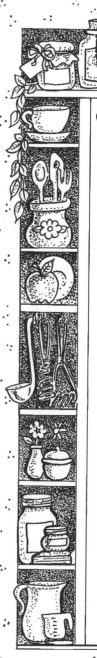

CHICKEN CRESCENT SANDWICHES

3 oz cream cheese, softened
2 tbsp butter, melted

2 cups chicken, cooked & chopped
2 tbsp chives
1 tbsp pimento
2 tbsp milk
salt to taste
pepper to taste

8-oz tube refrigerated crescent rolls

1 tbsp butter, melted
¾ cup seasoned croutons, crushed

PREPARE – Blend cream cheese with 2 tablespoons melted butter until smooth. Add next 6 ingredients and mix well. Separate dough into 4 squares and press perforations to seal. Spoon ½ cup mixture onto center of each square. Pull corners to center and twist to seal. Brush tops with melted butter and sprinkle with crushed croutons. Place on buttered baking sheet.

BAKE – Bake at 350° for 20-25 minutes.

Kim Bulger – Staff

HOT FOCACCIA SANDWICH

1 round loaf focaccia bread
mayonnaise
¼ lb or more sliced meat of choice
¼ lb or more sliced cheese of choice

spaghetti sauce

PREPARE – Cut bread in half like a layered cake. Spread mayonnaise on each half. Layer on the meat and cheese. Replace top and wrap in foil.

BAKE – Bake at 250° for 30 minutes or until cheese is melted. Cut into wedges and serve with heated spaghetti sauce for dipping.

This recipe doesn't take much time away from quilting! It's also wonderful for simple party sandwiches.

Sandi Irish
Staff

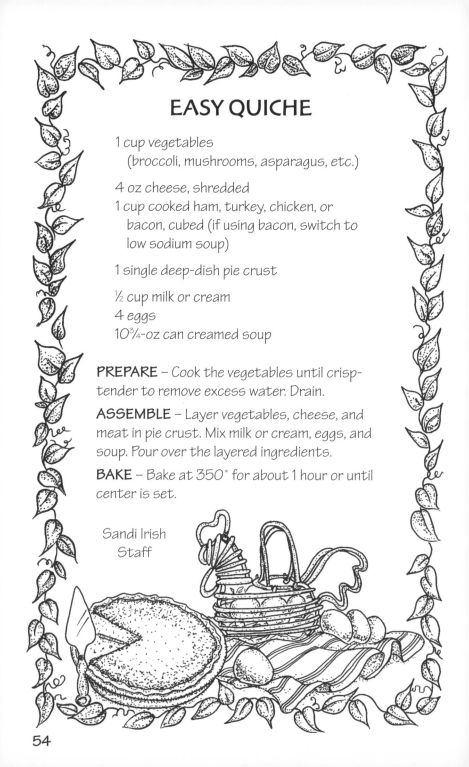

EASY QUICHE

1 cup vegetables
   (broccoli, mushrooms, asparagus, etc.)

4 oz cheese, shredded
1 cup cooked ham, turkey, chicken, or
   bacon, cubed (if using bacon, switch to
   low sodium soup)

1 single deep-dish pie crust

½ cup milk or cream
4 eggs
10¾-oz can creamed soup

PREPARE – Cook the vegetables until crisp-tender to remove excess water. Drain.

ASSEMBLE – Layer vegetables, cheese, and meat in pie crust. Mix milk or cream, eggs, and soup. Pour over the layered ingredients.

BAKE – Bake at 350° for about 1 hour or until center is set.

Sandi Irish
   Staff

54

QUICK CHICKEN-ZUCCHINI

2-3 medium zucchini
½ medium onion, chopped
2 medium tomatoes, chopped
2-3 chicken breasts, cooked & cubed
seasoned salt to taste
pepper to taste

Parmesan cheese, grated

SAUTÉ – Slice zucchini ⅛" thick, then halve the slices. Sauté zucchini and onion until crisp-tender. Add chopped tomatoes, chicken, seasoned salt, and pepper.

SERVE – Sprinkle with Parmesan and serve with French bread.

TIP – Substitute a 14½-oz can of stewed tomatoes for the fresh tomatoes.

A great "farmer's market" recipe. Any favorite veggies can be added. I add garlic and various herbs.

Sandi Irish
Staff

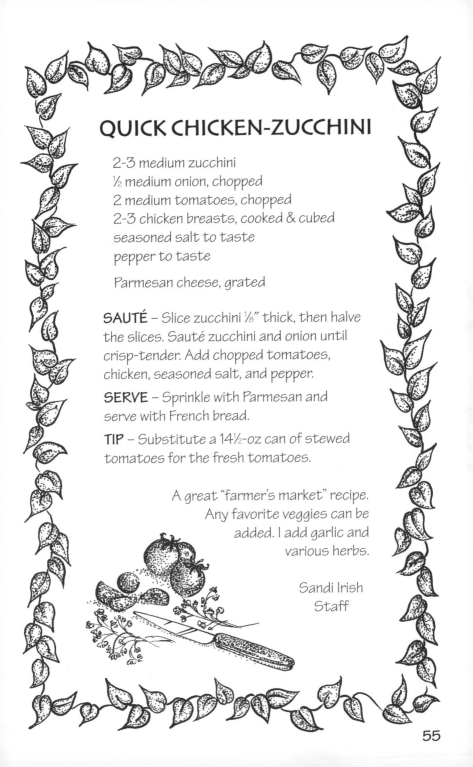

CROCK POT PORK ROAST

3-4 lb pork roast
   (boneless or bone-in)
¼ cup soy sauce
½ cup water

PREPARE – Brown roast on all sides. Place in crock pot and pour in soy sauce and water. Cover.

COOK – Cook at least 5 hours at high. Just before serving, remove the roast and thicken the gravy. Use gravy over rice or potatoes.

A great start-it-and-forget-it recipe given to me when my first baby was born. My neighbor prepared dinners for my husband and me for three nights. It was wonderful to just set the table and wait to see what they brought.

Helen Thorn

PineTree Lodge Designs,
Machine Quilting Teacher

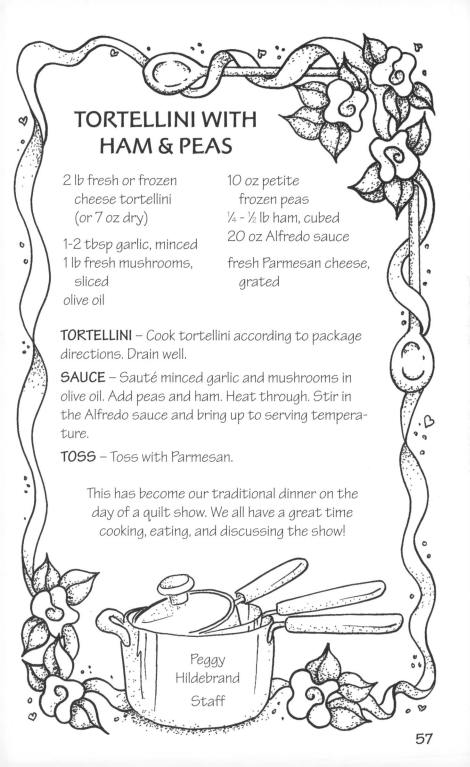

TORTELLINI WITH HAM & PEAS

2 lb fresh or frozen
   cheese tortellini
   (or 7 oz dry)

1-2 tbsp garlic, minced
1 lb fresh mushrooms,
   sliced
olive oil

10 oz petite
   frozen peas
¼ - ½ lb ham, cubed
20 oz Alfredo sauce

fresh Parmesan cheese,
   grated

TORTELLINI – Cook tortellini according to package directions. Drain well.

SAUCE – Sauté minced garlic and mushrooms in olive oil. Add peas and ham. Heat through. Stir in the Alfredo sauce and bring up to serving temperature.

TOSS – Toss with Parmesan.

This has become our traditional dinner on the day of a quilt show. We all have a great time cooking, eating, and discussing the show!

Peggy
Hildebrand
Staff

SPAGHETTI PIE

6 oz spaghetti
2 tbsp margarine
⅓ cup Parmesan, grated
2 eggs, well beaten

1 lb ground beef
½ cup onion, chopped
¼ cup green pepper, chopped

8-oz can tomatoes, undrained, cut up

6-oz can tomato paste
1 tsp sugar
1 tsp dried oregano
½ tsp garlic salt

1 cup ricotta

½ cup mozzarella, shredded

CRUST – Cook and drain spaghetti. Stir margarine, Parmesan, and eggs into hot spaghetti. Form mixture into a crust in buttered 10" pie plate.

FILLING – Brown ground beef. Drain fat. Add onion and green pepper. Sauté until tender. Stir in tomatoes, tomato paste, sugar, oregano, and garlic salt. Simmer 10 minutes. Spread ricotta over crust. Fill with tomato mixture. Cover edge of spaghetti with foil.

BAKE – Bake uncovered at 350° for 20 minutes. Sprinkle with mozzarella. Bake 5 minutes more.

This recipe for spaghetti pie was given to me so many years ago I cannot remember who shared it. It has become a tried-and-true family and quilting favorite, sort of a combination of lasagna and spaghetti. I usually replace the meat with fresh steamed vegetables. It is great for assembling ahead of time and baking at the last minute.

Jean Humenansky
Owner

"THE BEST COOKIES I EVER ATE"

2 cups butter
2 cups sugar
2 cups brown sugar
2 tsp vanilla
4 eggs

5 cups oatmeal
4 cups flour

1 tsp salt
2 tsp baking powder
2 tsp baking soda

24 oz chocolate chips
7-oz chocolate bar, grated
3 cups nuts, chopped

CREAM – Cream first 4 ingredients until light and fluffy. Add eggs 1 at a time, beating after each addition.

MIX – Process oatmeal to a flour in blender. Whisk oatmeal flour with the next 4 ingredients. Add to creamed mixture and stir.

ADD – Stir in chocolate and nuts.

BAKE – Drop on cookie sheet 2" apart. Bake at 375° for 6 minutes.

MAKES – 112 cookies

Next to crispy rice squares, these cookies rate #1 with my three grandsons, Matthew, Bradley, and Kevin.

Jean Humenansky – Owner

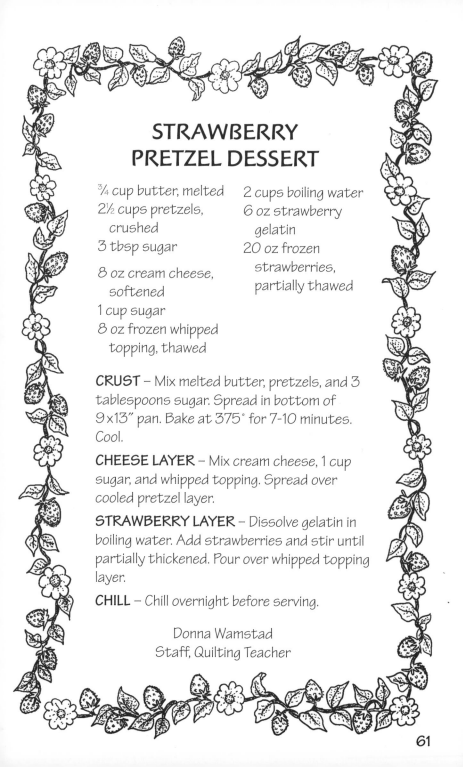

STRAWBERRY PRETZEL DESSERT

¾ cup butter, melted
2½ cups pretzels, crushed
3 tbsp sugar

8 oz cream cheese, softened
1 cup sugar
8 oz frozen whipped topping, thawed

2 cups boiling water
6 oz strawberry gelatin
20 oz frozen strawberries, partially thawed

CRUST – Mix melted butter, pretzels, and 3 tablespoons sugar. Spread in bottom of 9x13" pan. Bake at 375° for 7-10 minutes. Cool.

CHEESE LAYER – Mix cream cheese, 1 cup sugar, and whipped topping. Spread over cooled pretzel layer.

STRAWBERRY LAYER – Dissolve gelatin in boiling water. Add strawberries and stir until partially thickened. Pour over whipped topping layer.

CHILL – Chill overnight before serving.

Donna Wamstad
Staff, Quilting Teacher

FRESH FRUIT PIZZA

1 cup flour
½ cup butter
¼ cup powdered sugar

8 oz cream cheese,
softened
⅓ cup sugar
1 tsp vanilla

1 cup pineapple juice
1 tsp lemon juice
½ cup sugar
2 tbsp cornstarch

2-4 fresh seasonal fruits
20-oz can pineapple
rings, drained

CRUST – Mix flour, butter and powdered sugar. Press into a pizza pan or 9 x13" jelly roll pan. Bake at 350° for 15 minutes. Cool.

FILLING – Mix cream cheese, ⅓ cup sugar and vanilla. Spread on cooled crust.

GLAZE – Mix juices, ½ cup sugar, and cornstarch in saucepan. Cook and stir until thick. Cool.

ASSEMBLE – Wash and slice fresh fruits. Arrange fruit, including pineapple rings, over filling. Pour cooled glaze over fruit. When using bananas, apples, or peaches, completely cover with glaze to prevent discoloring. Chill until time to serve.

Laurie Toensing
Staff, Teacher, Machine Quilter

RICH & CHOCOLATE-Y CHEESECAKE DESSERT

2 cups wafer cookie crumbs
  (chocolate or vanilla)
6 tbsp butter, melted

14 oz caramels
¼ cup milk
1 cup pecans, chopped

16 oz cream cheese,
  softened
½ cup sugar
1 tsp vanilla
2 eggs
4 squares semisweet chocolate,
  melted

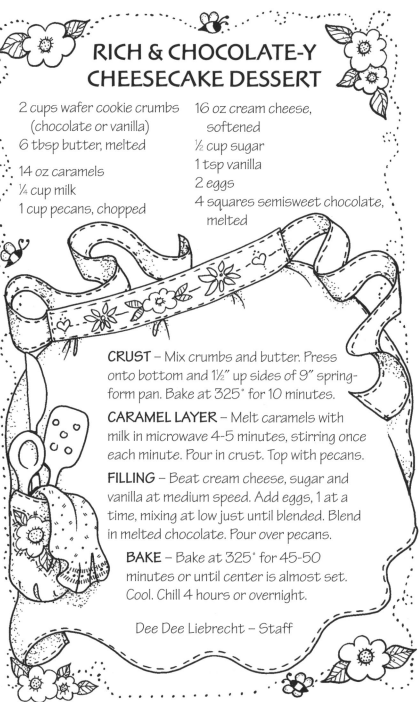

CRUST – Mix crumbs and butter. Press onto bottom and 1½" up sides of 9" springform pan. Bake at 325° for 10 minutes.

CARAMEL LAYER – Melt caramels with milk in microwave 4-5 minutes, stirring once each minute. Pour in crust. Top with pecans.

FILLING – Beat cream cheese, sugar and vanilla at medium speed. Add eggs, 1 at a time, mixing at low just until blended. Blend in melted chocolate. Pour over pecans.

BAKE – Bake at 325° for 45-50 minutes or until center is almost set. Cool. Chill 4 hours or overnight.

Dee Dee Liebrecht – Staff

QUILTING HINTS

I keep a stack of 2½" squares next to my sewing machine when I am piecing. Instead of using a scrap as a runner when I begin and end, I piece the 2½" squares into four-patch squares, and before I know it, I have enough for a small quilt. Using a runner square saves thread and prevents the machine from "eating" the points of triangles and squares. **Kim Bulger**

If having problems getting motivated, set a small goal. For example: "In the next twenty minutes, I will have my first block sewn together." Before you know it, three blocks will be done. **Ann Palmer**

I thread several needles onto one spool of thread in the morning when it is easier to see the small eyes of the needles. I slide one needle down at a time and cut off the amount of thread I need. I always knot the freshly cut end. **Peggy Hildebrand**

If you ever win a ribbon for one of your quilts, use it as leverage for fabric purchases, as in "Honey, I need this fabric. After all, I am an award-winning quilter, and I do have a standard to maintain". This also will help you garner a new sewing machine, tables, better lighting, and so on. **Sandi Irish**

Country Stitches

2200 Coolidge Road, East Lansing, Michigan 48823
Phone: 517-351-2416 Fax: 517-351-3051
E-mail: stitches@countrystitches.com
Web Address: www.countrystitches.com

Country Stitches

Located only a block from one major highway and within five miles of two others, Country Stitches draws customers from all over Michigan as well as northern Indiana and Ohio. Known for its extensive class schedule and a large annual post-Labor Day quilt show, Festival of Quilts, the shop is one of the largest in the country.

The owner of Country Stitches, Anita Covert, the wife of a sixth-generation dairy farmer, strives to maintain a small shop atmosphere that puts the customer first. In spite of having earned three advanced university degrees, it is Anita's experience as a nursery school teacher that she cites as the most important to her nine-teen-year-old quilt shop business. Overseeing 55 salespeople, 1500 classes per year, one of the two largest Viking dealerships in the U.S., and producing sewing machine books for Viking, requires knowing "where everyone is and what everyone is doing"!

Country Stitches has been called a quilter's heaven since they have what quilters want—plenty of cotton fabric (over 7000 bolts), the latest gadgets, books, patterns, and kits. Also available in the shop are fashion fabrics, unique gift items, and a large counted-thread inventory. Don't miss Country Stitches when you're in Lansing, Michigan!

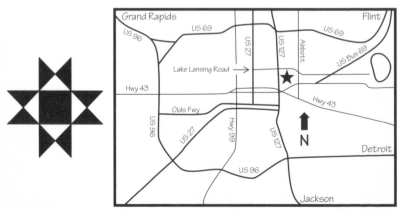

Take Lake Lansing Road exit, east, off US 127
2200 Coolidge Road

OLD-FASHIONED LEMONADE

1¼ cups fresh lemon juice
¾ cup sugar
4¼ cups cold water
lemon slices

MIX – Stir lemon juice and sugar in large pitcher until sugar dissolves. Add cold water and lemon slices. Stir well.
CHILL – Chill. Serve over ice.

A refreshing drink for a break during quilting.

Susan Sterle
Systems Manager

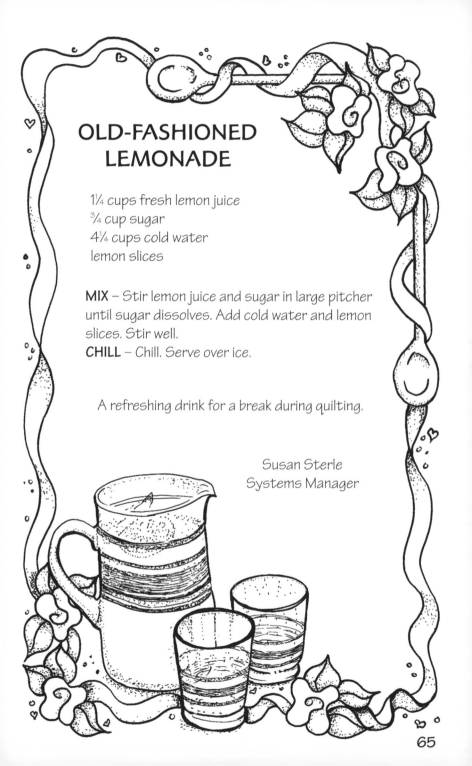

NACHO DIP

12 oz sour cream
8 oz cream cheese,
  softened
1 package (1¼-oz)
  taco seasoning
  mix

lettuce, shredded
tomatoes, chopped

cheddar or Monterey
  Jack cheese, grated

crackers or chips

MIX – Mix first 3 ingredients until smooth.
SPREAD – Spread cream cheese mixture on plate and layer lettuce, tomatoes, and cheese on top.
SERVE – Serve with crackers or chips.

Brian developed this dip as a
great postgame snack.

Brian Ladson
Vice President

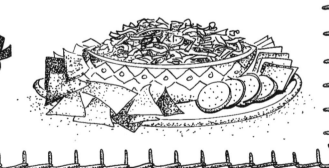

66

CHICKEN WINGS

Anita Covert
President, Owner

| chicken wings | Worcestershire sauce |
| soy sauce | grenadine syrup |

MARINATE – Marinate wings overnight in equal parts soy sauce and Worcestershire sauce.

BAKE – Bake at 350° for 15 minutes. Cover with grenadine. Bake another 30 minutes. Turn wings to cover with glaze. Bake 45-60 minutes.

These wings are a perennial favorite at the Country Stitches holiday party.

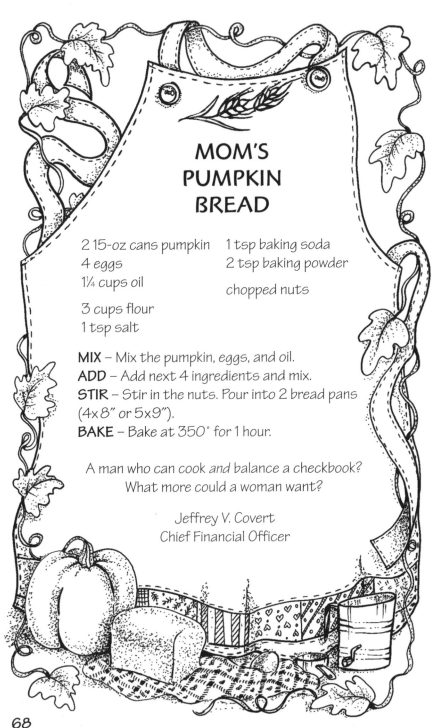

MOM'S PUMPKIN BREAD

2 15-oz cans pumpkin
4 eggs
1¼ cups oil

3 cups flour
1 tsp salt

1 tsp baking soda
2 tsp baking powder

chopped nuts

MIX – Mix the pumpkin, eggs, and oil.
ADD – Add next 4 ingredients and mix.
STIR – Stir in the nuts. Pour into 2 bread pans (4x8" or 5x9").
BAKE – Bake at 350° for 1 hour.

A man who can cook *and* balance a checkbook?
What more could a woman want?

Jeffrey V. Covert
Chief Financial Officer

PAULA'S FABULOUS CINNAMON ROLLS

2 loaves frozen bread,
   defrosted
½ cup butter, melted
½ cup white sugar
¾ cup brown sugar
cinnamon

Frosting:
1½ cups powdered sugar
3 tbsp butter
3 tsp vanilla
milk, enough to make
   frosting thin

FORM ROLLS – Roll bread dough to approximately 11 x 14″ and ⅜″ thick. Spread half of butter over dough. Sprinkle sugars over butter, then dust generously with cinnamon. Roll up and cut into 1″ slices and place in buttered 11 x 14″ cake pan.

LET RISE & BAKE – Cover and let rise until they are almost double in size. Bake at 350° for 20 minutes, then check. They may need to bake up to 5 minutes more, until just golden brown. If they bake too long, they get hard! Brush tops with remaining butter, then turn out on cooling rack.

FROST – Mix frosting ingredients well. When rolls are almost cool, turn them over on a tray and frost.

VARIATIONS – Add nuts and/or maple syrup to the bottom of the pan. Add boiled raisins to the sugars. Use orange juice, amaretto, or maple syrup as part of the liquid in the frosting.

A treat that's truly
legendary in our store!

Paula Cole
Instructor

MAKE-AHEAD MASHED POTATOES

10 medium potatoes, peeled and quartered

8 oz cream cheese, softened
½ cup butter
1 cup hot milk

COOK – Cook potatoes in salted water until tender. Drain. Add remaining ingredients and beat vigorously with electric mixer.

FILL CASSEROLE – Spray large casserole with cooking spray and fill with potatoes. May be refrigerated at this point for use the following day.

BAKE – Remove from refrigerator one hour before serving time. Bake at 350° for one hour or at 425° for 45 minutes.

SERVINGS – 10-12

Cut down on holiday work by making the potatoes the day before.

Marilyn Davidson
Shop Manager

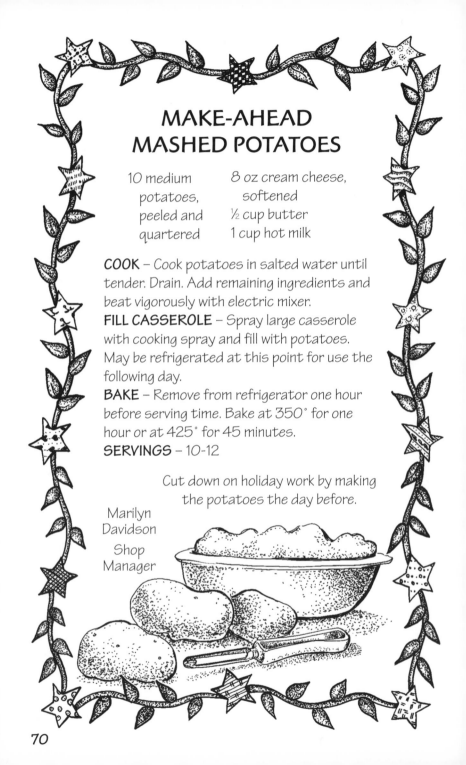

70

SAVORY BEEF STEW

2 lb stewing beef, cut
   into 1" cubes
¼ cup vegetable oil

1½ cups onion, chopped
14½-oz can tomatoes
3 tbsp quick tapioca
10½-oz can beef broth
1 clove garlic, minced
1 tbsp parsley flakes
2½ tsp salt

¼ tsp pepper
1 bay leaf

6 medium carrots, cut
   into strips
3 medium potatoes,
   quartered
½ cup celery, chopped

15-oz can peas
(optional)

BROWN – Brown beef in oil.

ADD – Add next 9 ingredients and bring to a boil.

TRANSFER – Transfer to 3-quart casserole with cover.

BAKE – Bake, covered, at 350° for 1½ hours, or until meat is tender. Bake up to an extra hour to make the meat even more tender.

ADD – Add carrots, potatoes, and celery.

BAKE – Bake 1 hour. If adding canned peas, add 15 minutes before serving. Remove bay leaf before serving.

SERVE – Serve with French bread.

Marilyn Davidson
Shop Manager

POTATO-CRUST QUICHE

3 medium potatoes
¼ cup butter or margarine

2 cups loose-pack frozen
   mixed vegetables
½ cup cheddar, shredded

2 eggs, beaten
5½-oz can evaporated milk
¼ tsp salt
⅛ tsp pepper

1 tbsp fine dry bread
   crumbs or toasted
   wheat germ

carrot curls
parsley sprigs

CRUST – Cook potatoes, covered, in boiling water until tender. Drain, peel. Mash with a potato masher. Measure 1⅓ cups. Stir in butter or margarine. Spoon into buttered 9″ pie plate. Spread over bottom and up sides of plate, building up sides with a spoon.

FILLING – Arrange vegetables in bottom of potato crust; sprinkle with cheese. In a small bowl, combine eggs, milk, salt, and pepper; pour over cheese. Sprinkle with bread crumbs or wheat germ.

BAKE – Bake at 375° for 40-50 minutes. Garnish with carrot curls and parsley.

TIP – Substitute instant mashed potatoes for the fresh ones.

As a newlywed and a working woman, I am always looking for tasty recipes that are quick and easy, but I also want something good for us.

Jasmin Pace
Secretary

HAMBURGER BARLEY SOUP

1 lb hamburger,
  browned

2 cups vegetables,
  at least 3 kinds

2 28-oz cans
  tomatoes

1 bay leaf
1 onion, chopped
salt & pepper
  to taste

¼ cup barley

BROWN – Brown and drain hamburger.
COOK – Put hamburger into pot with all other ingredients except barley. Cook on low heat until all veggies are done, 20 minutes or longer.
SIMMER – Add barley and simmer on low for 40 minutes or until barley is done.

This easy soup gives you more time
for sewing and quilting.

Deb VanAken
Instructor

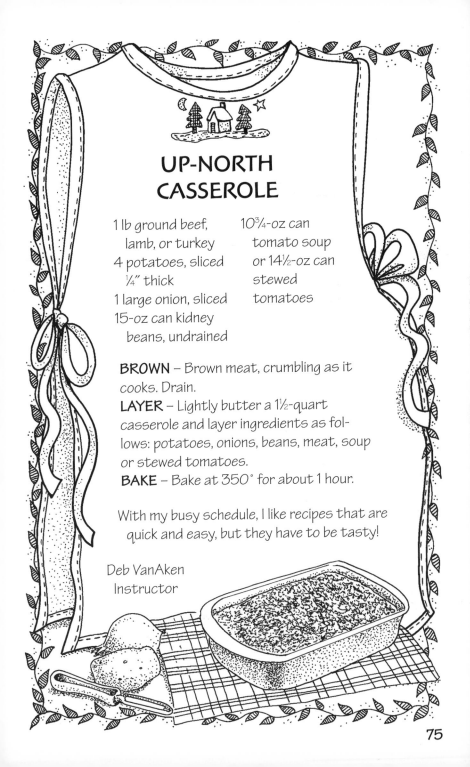

UP-NORTH CASSEROLE

1 lb ground beef,
  lamb, or turkey
4 potatoes, sliced
  ¼" thick
1 large onion, sliced
15-oz can kidney
  beans, undrained

10¾-oz can
  tomato soup
  or 14½-oz can
  stewed
  tomatoes

BROWN – Brown meat, crumbling as it cooks. Drain.

LAYER – Lightly butter a 1½-quart casserole and layer ingredients as follows: potatoes, onions, beans, meat, soup or stewed tomatoes.

BAKE – Bake at 350° for about 1 hour.

With my busy schedule, I like recipes that are quick and easy, but they have to be tasty!

Deb VanAken
Instructor

SALMON SUPPER PIE

1⅔ cups flour
½ tsp salt
⅛ tsp cayenne pepper
1 cup cheddar cheese,
   grated
½ cup shortening
5-6 tbsp ice water

14¾-oz can salmon
10 oz frozen or fresh
   steamed broccoli
2 tbsp onion, finely
   chopped

2 tbsp margarine
1 tbsp flour
10¾-oz can cream of
   celery soup
¾ cup milk

2 tsp lemon juice
2 hard cooked eggs,
   diced
½ tsp Worcestershire
   sauce
2 tbsp minced parsley

PASTRY – Combine flour, salt, pepper, and cheese. Cut in shortening. Add ice water 1 tbsp at a time until dough holds together. Divide pastry in half. Set aside half for lattice top and line 9" pie plate with other half.

FILLING – Drain salmon, reserving liquid. Break salmon into very small pieces. Cut broccoli into pieces. Sauté onion in margarine. Blend in flour, then salmon liquid, soup, and milk, stirring constantly until thick and smooth. Blend lemon juice, eggs, Worcestershire, and parsley into soup mixture. Arrange half the salmon and broccoli in pie shell, cover with half the soup mixture. Repeat. Put on lattice top.

BAKE – Bake at 400° for 40-50 minutes. If crust gets too brown, reduce heat.

Geri Jastram – Staff

CAKE TO DIE FOR

1 orange cake mix
½ cup sour cream
2 eggs
21-oz can peach pie
   filling

3 oz instant vanilla
   pudding mix

8 oz cream cheese,
   softened
20-oz can crushed
   pineapple
8 oz frozen whipped
   topping, thawed

MIX – Combine cake mix and next 3 ingredients with a fork and pour into a jelly roll pan.
BAKE – Bake at 350° for 35 minutes. Cool.
TOPPING – Beat pudding into cream cheese. Mix in pineapple. Fold in whipped topping. Spread on cake.

I got the recipe from an aunt and fell in love with the ease of such a yummy dessert. I altered it slightly and renamed it to describe it more accurately!

Doreen Trevena
Office Manager

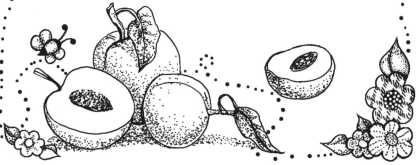

POPCORN BALLS

1½-2 cups unpopped popcorn

⅔ cup white corn syrup
2 tbsp water
1 lb powdered sugar
10 large marshmallows
¼ cup margarine

POP – Pop the popcorn. Air-popped is best!
MIX – Mix remaining ingredients and heat until melted. Pour onto popcorn. Form into balls.
STORE – Store in plastic baggies.

Cherie developed this recipe to make popcorn balls that were soft and easy on the teeth.

Cherie Sterle
Mother of Susan Sterle
Systems Manager

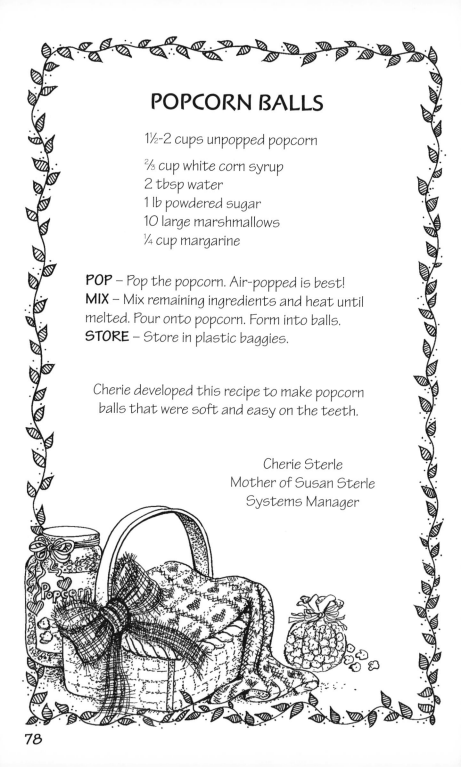

APPLESAUCE COOKIES

2 scant cups sugar
1 cup shortening
2 eggs

1 tsp cloves
1 tsp nutmeg
1 tsp salt

3½ cups flour
1 tsp baking powder
2 tsp baking soda
2 tsp cinnamon

2 cups quick rolled oats
2 cups applesauce

1 cup chopped nuts
1 cup raisins

CREAM – Cream sugar and shortening. Stir in eggs.

SIFT – Sift flour, baking powder, baking soda, cinnamon, cloves, nutmeg, and salt.

ADD – Add flour mixture and oats to creamed mixture alternately with applesauce. Beat well. Stir in nuts and raisins.

LET SET – Let set for about an hour to let oats soak up excess moisture. Drop onto a buttered baking sheet.

BAKE – Bake at 350° for 10-15 minutes.

This is my grandmother's recipe. Often Mom will bake up a batch and send them to the store still warm from the oven. My students call them breakfast cookies.

Pam Smolek
Manager

MELT-IN-YOUR-MOUTH NO-BAKE COOKIES

2 cups sugar
½ cup milk
½ cup butter
1 tbsp cocoa

½ cup peanut butter
1½-2 cups quick-
   cooking oatmeal

BOIL – Bring first 4 ingredients to a boil. Boil for exactly 60 seconds. Remove from heat.
ADD – Add peanut butter and stir until melted. Add oatmeal. Stir until well blended.
DROP – Drop onto wax paper.

I like cookies to melt in my mouth. Less cocoa and oatmeal and boiling for only one minute makes it happen!

Ann Covert Drane
Director of Education

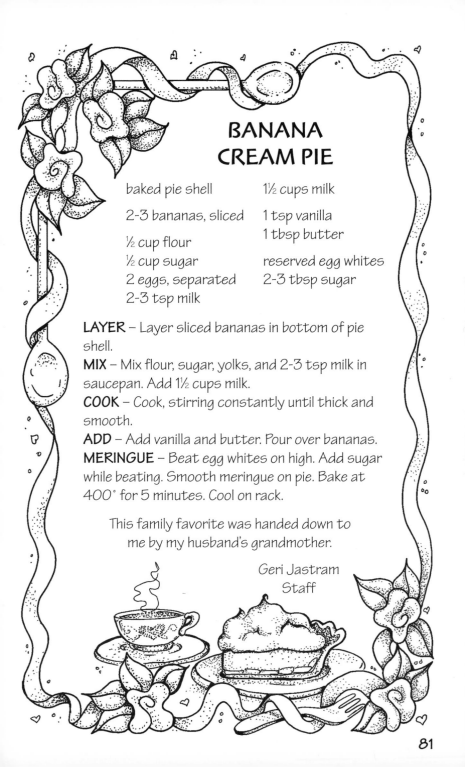

BANANA CREAM PIE

baked pie shell

2-3 bananas, sliced

½ cup flour
½ cup sugar
2 eggs, separated
2-3 tsp milk

1½ cups milk

1 tsp vanilla
1 tbsp butter

reserved egg whites
2-3 tbsp sugar

LAYER – Layer sliced bananas in bottom of pie shell.

MIX – Mix flour, sugar, yolks, and 2-3 tsp milk in saucepan. Add 1½ cups milk.

COOK – Cook, stirring constantly until thick and smooth.

ADD – Add vanilla and butter. Pour over bananas.

MERINGUE – Beat egg whites on high. Add sugar while beating. Smooth meringue on pie. Bake at 400° for 5 minutes. Cool on rack.

This family favorite was handed down to me by my husband's grandmother.

Geri Jastram
Staff

81

DUTCH APPLE PIE

Crust:
1 cup flour
½ tsp salt
⅓ cup shortening
2-3 tbsp ice water

Filling:
5-6 cups cooking apples,
    peeled & sliced
1 tbsp lemon juice
¾ cup sugar
1 tsp cinnamon
⅛ tsp salt

Topping:
1 cup flour
½ cup sugar
⅓ cup butter

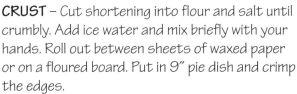

CRUST – Cut shortening into flour and salt until crumbly. Add ice water and mix briefly with your hands. Roll out between sheets of waxed paper or on a floured board. Put in 9" pie dish and crimp the edges.

FILLING – Mix filling ingredients until apples are well coated. Put into unbaked pie shell.

TOPPING – Cut butter into flour and sugar until crumbly. Sprinkle over top of apples in pie crust.

BAKE – Bake at 400° for 20 minutes. Reduce temperature to 350° and bake an additional 40 minutes or until apples are cooked and topping is lightly browned. If topping appears to be getting overly brown, place a folded aluminum foil tent lightly over the pie.

Mom made this often in the summertime when I was growing up and always topped it with vanilla ice cream. After I was married, Mom and I would often make the pie together. It is the greatest compliment for me when my husband tells me it tastes just like hers.

Nancy Willenbrink
Staff

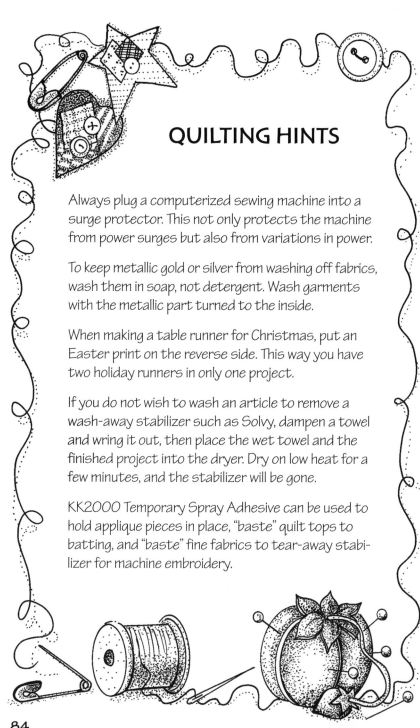

QUILTING HINTS

Always plug a computerized sewing machine into a surge protector. This not only protects the machine from power surges but also from variations in power.

To keep metallic gold or silver from washing off fabrics, wash them in soap, not detergent. Wash garments with the metallic part turned to the inside.

When making a table runner for Christmas, put an Easter print on the reverse side. This way you have two holiday runners in only one project.

If you do not wish to wash an article to remove a wash-away stabilizer such as Solvy, dampen a towel and wring it out, then place the wet towel and the finished project into the dryer. Dry on low heat for a few minutes, and the stabilizer will be gone.

KK2000 Temporary Spray Adhesive can be used to hold applique pieces in place, "baste" quilt tops to batting, and "baste" fine fabrics to tear-away stabilizer for machine embroidery.

The Fabric Patch

5436 D Arrow Highway, Montclair, California 91763
Phone: 909-985-9000 Fax: 909-985-9163
E-mail: carolyn@thefabricpatch.com
Web Address: www.thefabricpatch.com

The Fabric Patch

Packed with every quilt-related item imaginable, The Fabric Patch, in southern California off Interstate 10, serves a clientele ranging from the Mexican border to the Canadian. Carolyn Reese and her mother, Marie White, opened the shop in 1981, and their new life blossomed. The shop now employs an average of 18 people. "Regulars" come from as far away as Saudi Arabia and Washington D.C. Carolyn enjoys a national reputation as a vendor at quilt shows from California to Kentucky. She has the satisfaction of having younger family members play an active role in her business.

Teachers with areas of expertise such as quilts from the 1930s, embellished clothing, and dolls of all kinds add to the charm and vitality of The Fabric Patch. The shop is also home base for the Road to California Quilters' Conference held annually in January at the Ontario, California Convention Center.

The Fabric Patch is known for its large inventory, including a unique sliding display for over 1000 pattern fronts. In addition to hundreds of quilting books, the shop carries children's picture books with quilt themes and an adult mystery series by a local author who uses quilt patterns in her book titles. Include The Fabric Patch in your next visit to southern California!

5436 D Arrow Highway

PECAN CHEESE BALL

8 oz cream cheese, softened

8½-oz can crushed pineapple, drained
1 cup pecans, chopped
¼ cup celery, chopped
1 tbsp onion, chopped (dried is OK)
½ tsp seasoned salt

pecans, chopped

PREPARE – Gradually stir drained pineapple, pecans, celery, onion and salt into cream cheese. Form into a ball and chill at least 4 hours.
GARNISH – Garnish with extra pecans. This keeps quite well and actually is better if made a day ahead.

Great for filling up hungry husbands when you just have to finish that last row of stitching!

Merle Edgar
Staff

SUE'S CRAB MELTAWAYS

8 oz sharp cheddar, grated
6 tbsp margarine
2 tbsp lemon juice

8 oz crabmeat (frozen imitation
   crab is okay)

8 English muffins

PREPARE – Mix first 3 ingredients.
Add crabmeat. Split muffins and cut
into quarters. Spread crabmeat
mixture on muffins.
BROIL – Broil until cheese melts.

A recipe from my friend, Sue Hale.

Cathy Norell
Staff

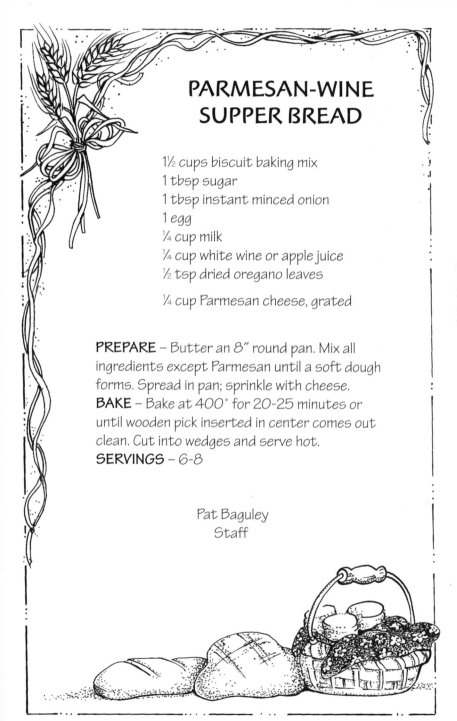

PARMESAN-WINE SUPPER BREAD

1½ cups biscuit baking mix
1 tbsp sugar
1 tbsp instant minced onion
1 egg
¼ cup milk
¼ cup white wine or apple juice
½ tsp dried oregano leaves

¼ cup Parmesan cheese, grated

PREPARE – Butter an 8″ round pan. Mix all ingredients except Parmesan until a soft dough forms. Spread in pan; sprinkle with cheese.
BAKE – Bake at 400° for 20-25 minutes or until wooden pick inserted in center comes out clean. Cut into wedges and serve hot.
SERVINGS – 6-8

Pat Baguley
Staff

RICE & ARTICHOKE SALAD

8-oz jar marinated artichokes
¼ cup mayonnaise

7-oz box chicken-flavored rice-vermicelli
   mix, cooked & cooled
4 scallions, chopped
½ cup green pepper, chopped
¼ - ½ cup green olives, sliced

PREPARE – Drain artichokes, reserving
marinade. Chop artichokes. Mix marinade
with mayonnaise.
TOSS – Toss all ingredients together.
TIP – Better made a day ahead. Add
chopped cooked chicken for a main dish.

Merle Edgar
Staff

PEAS & PEANUT SLAW

10 oz frozen peas, thawed
2 cups cabbage, finely shredded
1 green onion, thinly sliced

¼ cup sour cream
¼ cup mayonnaise
¼ tsp salt
¼ tsp curry powder
dash of pepper
1 tbsp prepared mustard
1 tbsp wine vinegar

¾ cup salted Spanish peanuts

SALAD – In a salad bowl, mix peas, cabbage, and onion.
DRESSING – In a small bowl, combine next 7 ingredients. Blend well.
TOSS – Pour over cabbage mixture and toss lightly. Cover and refrigerate for 1 hour or overnight.
GARNISH – Garnish with peanuts before serving.
SERVINGS – 4-6

Karen Rundlett
Staff

PASTA SALAD DELI-STYLE

½ lb rainbow rotini pasta, uncooked

1 small pepperoni stick, sliced
1 cup cauliflower flowerets
1 cup broccoli flowerets
1 cup Monterey Jack cheese, diced
½ cup green onions, sliced
½ cup Italian salad dressing

COOK – Cook rotini according to package directions. Drain. Cool.

COMBINE – In large bowl, combine remaining ingredients with rotini. Toss to coat with dressing.

CHILL – Cover and chill thoroughly. Toss gently before serving.

SERVINGS – 6-8

Kathy Zerbey
Staff

BUENOS DIAS BREAKFAST

12 eggs, beaten
½ cup flour
1 tsp baking powder
½ tsp salt
2 cups cottage cheese
1 lb Monterey Jack
   cheese, shredded

½ cup butter, melted
4 oz can diced green
   chiles

sour cream
salsa

MIX – Mix first 8 ingredients. Pour into 9 x 13" pan.
BAKE – Bake at 350° for 35 minutes.
SERVE – Serve with sour cream and salsa.

Cathy Norell
Staff

91

MEXICAN CHICKEN LASAGNA

2 tbsp salad oil
1 large onion, chopped
2 cloves garlic, minced or mashed
1 red or green bell pepper, seeded &
 chopped

2 10¾-oz cans condensed tomato
 soup
10-oz can enchilada sauce
1½ tsp salt
½ tsp pepper
4-12 tbsp chili powder
1 tsp ground cumin

2 cups small curd creamed cottage
 cheese
2 eggs
⅓ cup parsley, chopped
2-4 tbsp green chilies, diced

4 cups cooked chicken or turkey, torn
 into large pieces
10 oz lasagna noodles, cooked &
 drained
6 oz each cheddar & Monterey Jack
 cheese, sliced

sour cream

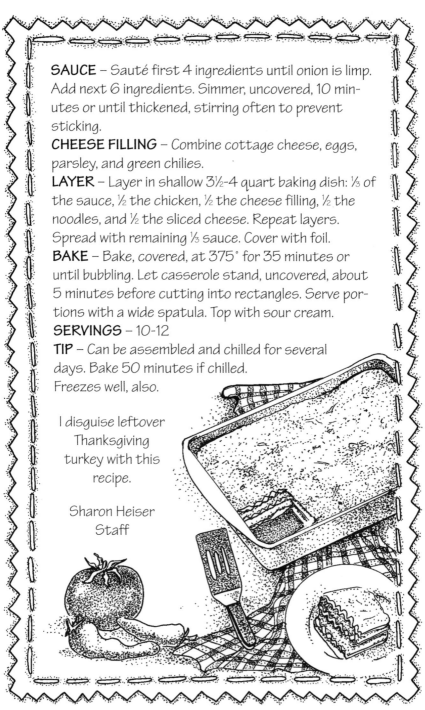

SAUCE – Sauté first 4 ingredients until onion is limp. Add next 6 ingredients. Simmer, uncovered, 10 minutes or until thickened, stirring often to prevent sticking.

CHEESE FILLING – Combine cottage cheese, eggs, parsley, and green chilies.

LAYER – Layer in shallow 3½-4 quart baking dish: ⅓ of the sauce, ½ the chicken, ½ the cheese filling, ½ the noodles, and ½ the sliced cheese. Repeat layers. Spread with remaining ⅓ sauce. Cover with foil.

BAKE – Bake, covered, at 375° for 35 minutes or until bubbling. Let casserole stand, uncovered, about 5 minutes before cutting into rectangles. Serve portions with a wide spatula. Top with sour cream.

SERVINGS – 10-12

TIP – Can be assembled and chilled for several days. Bake 50 minutes if chilled. Freezes well, also.

I disguise leftover Thanksgiving turkey with this recipe.

Sharon Heiser
Staff

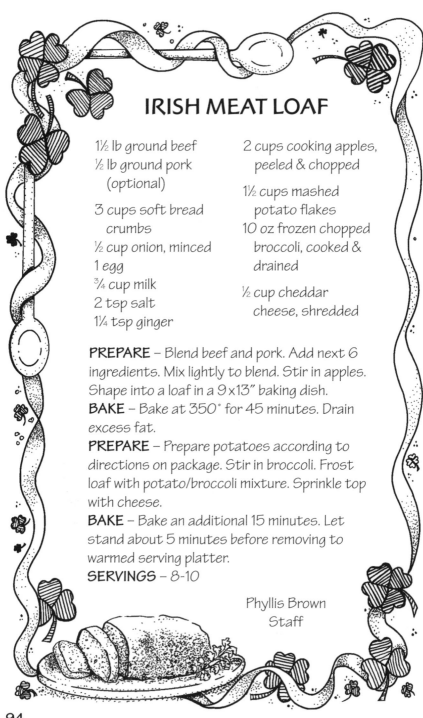

IRISH MEAT LOAF

1½ lb ground beef
½ lb ground pork
   (optional)

3 cups soft bread
   crumbs
½ cup onion, minced
1 egg
¾ cup milk
2 tsp salt
1¼ tsp ginger

2 cups cooking apples,
   peeled & chopped

1½ cups mashed
   potato flakes
10 oz frozen chopped
   broccoli, cooked &
   drained

½ cup cheddar
   cheese, shredded

PREPARE – Blend beef and pork. Add next 6 ingredients. Mix lightly to blend. Stir in apples. Shape into a loaf in a 9 x 13" baking dish.

BAKE – Bake at 350° for 45 minutes. Drain excess fat.

PREPARE – Prepare potatoes according to directions on package. Stir in broccoli. Frost loaf with potato/broccoli mixture. Sprinkle top with cheese.

BAKE – Bake an additional 15 minutes. Let stand about 5 minutes before removing to warmed serving platter.

SERVINGS – 8-10

Phyllis Brown
Staff

94

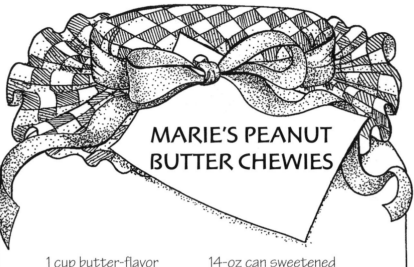

MARIE'S PEANUT BUTTER CHEWIES

1 cup butter-flavor
  shortening
1½ cups creamy peanut
  butter
1½ cups brown sugar,
  firmly packed

2 eggs

14-oz can sweetened
  condensed milk
2 tsp vanilla

2 cups all-purpose flour
1 tsp baking soda
1 tsp salt

1½ cups pecans, chopped

BEAT – Combine first 3 ingredients in large bowl. Beat at medium speed until well blended. Beat in next 3 ingredients.

COMBINE – Combine flour, soda, and salt. Mix into creamed mixture at low speed until just blended. Stir in nuts.

DROP – Drop 2 inches apart on baking sheet.

BAKE – Bake at 350° for 10-11 minutes or until lightly browned on bottom. Cool 2 minutes on baking sheet. Remove to cooling rack.

Marie White
Staff

CAROLYN'S PEANUT BRITTLE

2 cups raw Spanish peanuts

2 cups sugar
1 cup white corn syrup
1 cup water

dash of salt
3 tbsp butter
1 tsp vanilla
3 tsp baking soda

PREPARE – Place peanuts in the oven on a cookie sheet at 300°. Shake occasionally to roast evenly. Butter a large piece of heavy foil. To protect countertop from heat, place foil on several layers of newspaper.

COOK – Combine sugar, corn syrup, and water in heavy saucepan. Cook over medium-high heat, stirring constantly until sugar is dissolved. Continue to cook to soft ball stage, 236°. Remove peanuts from oven and stir into candy with salt. Continue cooking, stirring occasionally and watching carefully, until mixture reaches 300°. Remove from heat.

STIR – Stir in butter, then vanilla. Stir in soda and mix thoroughly. Mixture will foam. Pour onto prepared foil in an oval pattern. As the mixture cools, about 2-3 minutes, gently stretch the candy using a buttered fork. When cool, break into pieces and store in tightly closed container.

MAKES – 2½ lb

It just wouldn't be Christmas at our house without this peanut brittle.

Carolyn Reese
Owner

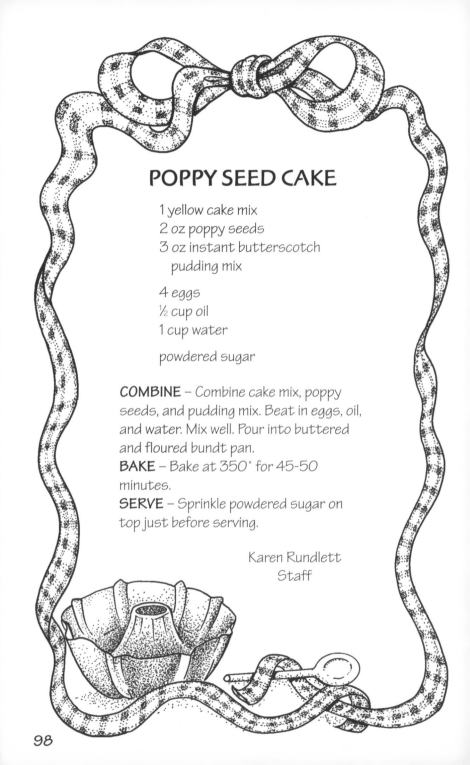

POPPY SEED CAKE

1 yellow cake mix
2 oz poppy seeds
3 oz instant butterscotch
  pudding mix

4 eggs
½ cup oil
1 cup water

powdered sugar

COMBINE – Combine cake mix, poppy seeds, and pudding mix. Beat in eggs, oil, and water. Mix well. Pour into buttered and floured bundt pan.
BAKE – Bake at 350° for 45-50 minutes.
SERVE – Sprinkle powdered sugar on top just before serving.

Karen Rundlett
Staff

STRAWBERRY DESSERT

1 large angel food cake, purchased
   or homemade

3 oz instant vanilla pudding mix
1 cup milk
1 pint vanilla ice cream, softened
3 oz strawberry gelatin
1 cup boiling water
16 oz frozen strawberries, thawed

whipped cream

LAYER – Rip apart cake and cover bottom of 9 x 13" pan. Blend pudding mix and milk. Add ice cream. Pour over cake. Dissolve gelatin in water. Add strawberries. Pour over cake.
CHILL – Chill. Garnish each serving with whipped cream.

Great in the summer—no cooking needed!

Merle Edgar
Staff

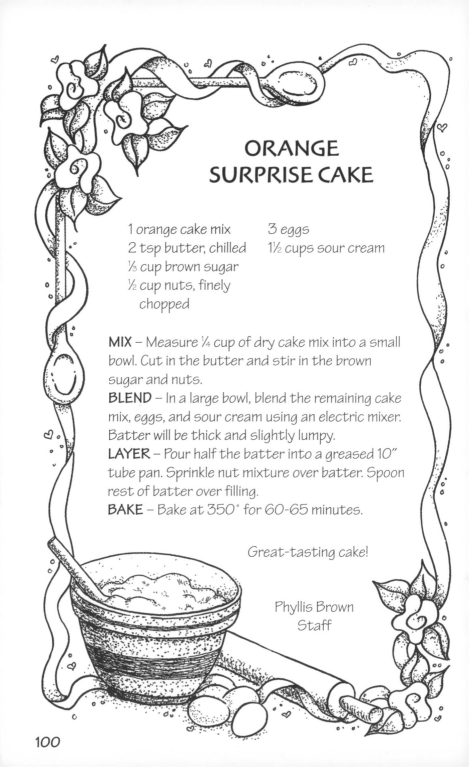

ORANGE SURPRISE CAKE

1 orange cake mix
2 tsp butter, chilled
⅓ cup brown sugar
½ cup nuts, finely
   chopped

3 eggs
1½ cups sour cream

MIX – Measure ¼ cup of dry cake mix into a small bowl. Cut in the butter and stir in the brown sugar and nuts.

BLEND – In a large bowl, blend the remaining cake mix, eggs, and sour cream using an electric mixer. Batter will be thick and slightly lumpy.

LAYER – Pour half the batter into a greased 10" tube pan. Sprinkle nut mixture over batter. Spoon rest of batter over filling.

BAKE – Bake at 350° for 60-65 minutes.

Great-tasting cake!

Phyllis Brown
Staff

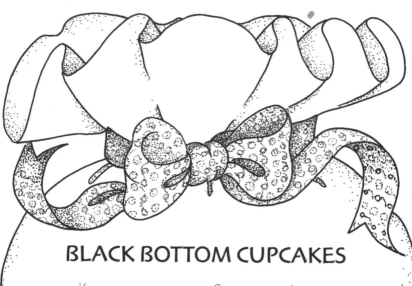

BLACK BOTTOM CUPCAKES

¼ cup cocoa
1 cup sugar
1¾ cups flour
1 tsp baking soda
1 egg
1 tsp white vinegar
1 cup oil
1 cup water

8 oz cream cheese, softened
1 tsp vanilla
1 egg, beaten
⅓ cup sugar
12 oz chocolate chips

sugar

BATTER – Mix first 8 ingredients until very smooth.
FILLING – Mix cream cheese, vanilla, egg, and sugar. Add chocolate chips.
LAYER – Fill cupcake papers halfway with batter. Put one tablespoon filling on each. Top with enough batter to cover the filling. Sprinkle with sugar.
BAKE – Bake at 350° for 25-30 minutes.
SERVINGS – 18

Kathy Zerbey
Staff

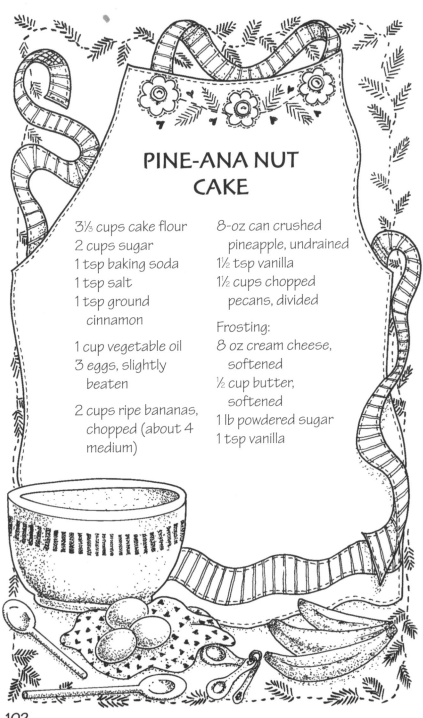

PINE-ANA NUT CAKE

3⅓ cups cake flour
2 cups sugar
1 tsp baking soda
1 tsp salt
1 tsp ground
    cinnamon

1 cup vegetable oil
3 eggs, slightly
    beaten

2 cups ripe bananas,
    chopped (about 4
    medium)

8-oz can crushed
    pineapple, undrained
1½ tsp vanilla
1½ cups chopped
    pecans, divided

Frosting:
8 oz cream cheese,
    softened
½ cup butter,
    softened
1 lb powdered sugar
1 tsp vanilla

102

MIX – In large bowl, mix first 5 ingredients. Add oil and eggs. Stir until dry ingredients are moistened. Do not beat! Stir in bananas, pineapple, vanilla, and 1 cup of pecans.

PREPARE – Butter and flour 3 round 9" cake pans. Divide batter evenly among the 3 pans.

BAKE – Bake at 350° for 25-30 minutes or until toothpick inserted in center comes out clean. Cool 10 minutes. Remove from pans and cool completely on wire racks.

FROSTING – Beat cream cheese and butter in large bowl on medium speed until smooth. Add powdered sugar and vanilla and beat until light and fluffy. Frost between layers. Frost top and sides. Sprinkle remaining pecans on top of cake.

A great cake for those who are allergic to chocolate or–gasp!– don't care for it.

Jane Vaughn
Staff

QUILTING HINTS

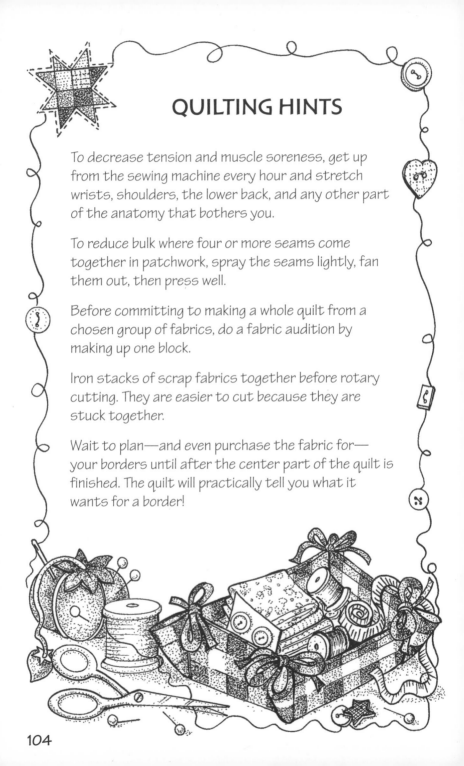

To decrease tension and muscle soreness, get up from the sewing machine every hour and stretch wrists, shoulders, the lower back, and any other part of the anatomy that bothers you.

To reduce bulk where four or more seams come together in patchwork, spray the seams lightly, fan them out, then press well.

Before committing to making a whole quilt from a chosen group of fabrics, do a fabric audition by making up one block.

Iron stacks of scrap fabrics together before rotary cutting. They are easier to cut because they are stuck together.

Wait to plan—and even purchase the fabric for—your borders until after the center part of the quilt is finished. The quilt will practically tell you what it wants for a border!

Little Quilts

1450-C Roswell Road, Marietta, Georgia 30062
Phone: 770-578-6727 Fax: 770-509-9748
E-mail: littlequilts@mindspring.com
Web Address: www.littlequilts.com

Little Quilts

Since 1986, Little Quilts has published patterns and booklets for "lovers of little things". Specializing in small, but not miniature, quilts based on traditional doll quilts from the past, these designs have had worldwide appeal.

Alice Berg, Mary Ellen Von Holt, and Sylvia Johnson are partners who also have coauthored books published by Martingale Publishing Co. — **Little Quilts All Through the House**, **Celebrate With Little Quilts**, **Living With Little Quilts**, and **Bunnies by the Bay Meet Little Quilts**. They also design a line of fabrics for Peter Pan® Fabrics.

By popular demand, they decided to open a retail store near the historic town of Marietta, Georgia. Located in a restored corn mill building built in 1947, the shop has a feeling of days gone by. It specializes in reproduction fabrics, rug hooking supplies, stitchery, and gifts for quilters. Everyone finds something when they visit. A highly trained staff is ready to assist. They invite you to "step into their world".

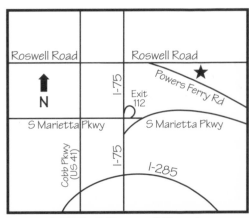

1450-C Roswell Road

ROASTED OLIVES IN FETA

1 cup pimento-stuffed olives

1 cup pitted ripe olives

3 tbsp Italian dressing

8 oz feta cheese, drained & crumbled

24 oz cream cheese, softened

½ teaspoon hot sauce

crackers

BAKE – Coat olives with dressing and spread on a 15 x 10 x 1" jellyroll pan. Bake at 400° for 25 minutes, being careful not to burn them. Cool.

COMBINE – Combine cheeses and hot sauce in large mixing bowl. Beat at medium speed until smooth. Coarsely chop roasted olives and stir into cheese mixture. Cover and chill at least 1 hour.

SHAPE – Shape into 2 balls. Serve with crackers.

MAKES – 4 cups

A "spiffy" Italian version of cream cheese and olive spread.

Fran House
Instructor

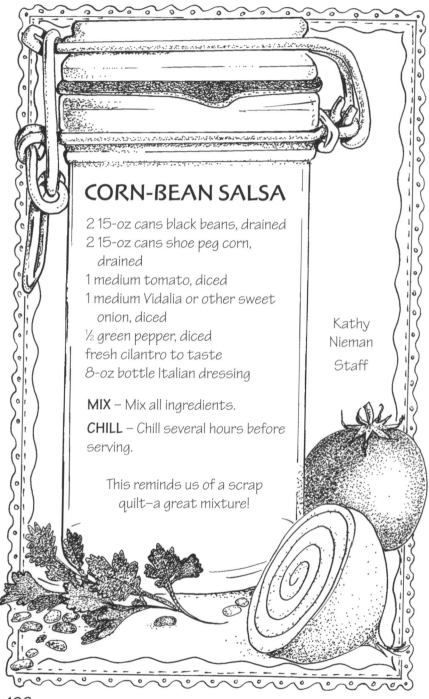

CORN-BEAN SALSA

2 15-oz cans black beans, drained
2 15-oz cans shoe peg corn,
   drained
1 medium tomato, diced
1 medium Vidalia or other sweet
   onion, diced
½ green pepper, diced
fresh cilantro to taste
8-oz bottle Italian dressing

Kathy
Nieman
Staff

MIX – Mix all ingredients.

CHILL – Chill several hours before
serving.

This reminds us of a scrap
quilt–a great mixture!

CHEESE & ONION BREAD

½ cup onion, chopped
2 tbsp butter

1 egg, beaten
½ cup milk
1½ cups biscuit mix

1 cup sharp cheese,
    shredded

2 tbsp dried parsley
½ tsp coarse pepper
pinch of salt

2 tbsp butter

SAUTÉ – Sauté onion in 2 tablespoons butter until tender but not brown.

MIX – Combine egg and milk. Stir into biscuit mix only until moist. Add onion, half of the cheese, parsley, pepper, and salt. Spread the mixture in a buttered 8" square pan. Sprinkle remaining cheese and butter on top.

BAKE – Bake at 400° for 20 minutes.

The aroma will bring them to the table!

Michelle Bautsch
Instructor

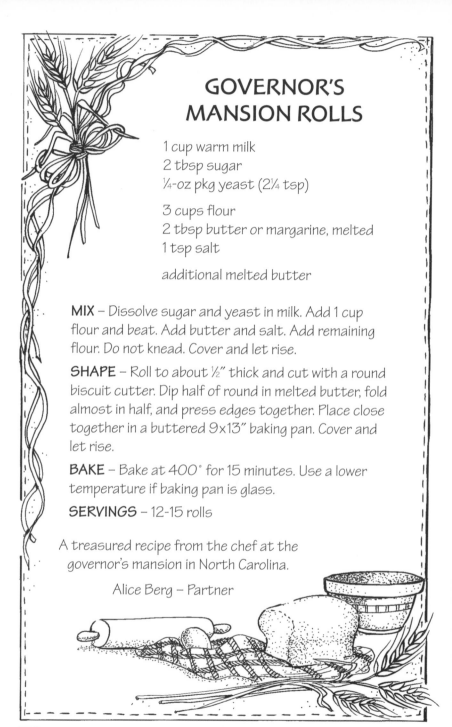

GOVERNOR'S MANSION ROLLS

1 cup warm milk
2 tbsp sugar
¼-oz pkg yeast (2¼ tsp)

3 cups flour
2 tbsp butter or margarine, melted
1 tsp salt

additional melted butter

MIX – Dissolve sugar and yeast in milk. Add 1 cup flour and beat. Add butter and salt. Add remaining flour. Do not knead. Cover and let rise.

SHAPE – Roll to about ½" thick and cut with a round biscuit cutter. Dip half of round in melted butter, fold almost in half, and press edges together. Place close together in a buttered 9x13" baking pan. Cover and let rise.

BAKE – Bake at 400° for 15 minutes. Use a lower temperature if baking pan is glass.

SERVINGS – 12-15 rolls

A treasured recipe from the chef at the governor's mansion in North Carolina.

Alice Berg – Partner

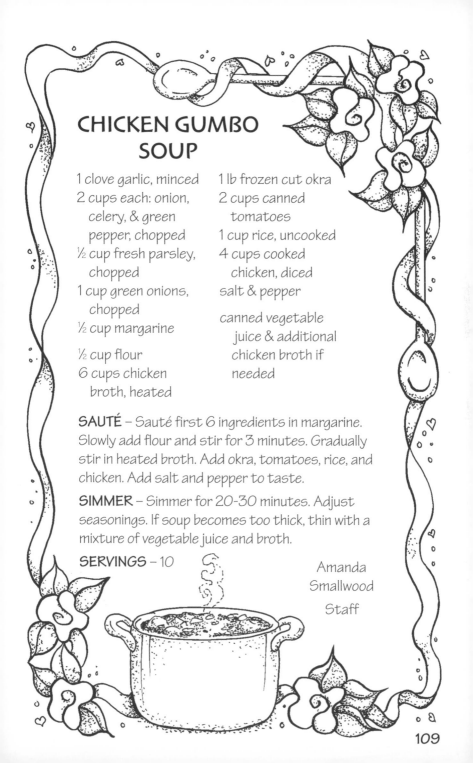

CHICKEN GUMBO SOUP

1 clove garlic, minced
2 cups each: onion, celery, & green pepper, chopped
½ cup fresh parsley, chopped
1 cup green onions, chopped
½ cup margarine

½ cup flour
6 cups chicken broth, heated

1 lb frozen cut okra
2 cups canned tomatoes
1 cup rice, uncooked
4 cups cooked chicken, diced
salt & pepper

canned vegetable juice & additional chicken broth if needed

SAUTÉ – Sauté first 6 ingredients in margarine. Slowly add flour and stir for 3 minutes. Gradually stir in heated broth. Add okra, tomatoes, rice, and chicken. Add salt and pepper to taste.

SIMMER – Simmer for 20-30 minutes. Adjust seasonings. If soup becomes too thick, thin with a mixture of vegetable juice and broth.

SERVINGS – 10

Amanda Smallwood

Staff

BROCCOLI SALAD

5 cups broccoli
  flowerets
½ cup raisins
¼ cup red onion,
  chopped

1 cup sunflower
  seeds
10 slices bacon,
  cooked &
  crumbled

2 tbsp sugar
3 tbsp vinegar
1 cup mayonnaise

MIX – Mix first 3 ingredients in a salad bowl. Blend next 3 ingredients.

TOSS – Toss salad and dressing. Chill until serving time.

TOP – Top with sunflower seeds and bacon.

Jennifer
Suter
Staff

110

FROZEN FRUIT SALAD

¼ cup sugar
1½ tbsp flour
½ tsp salt
¾ cup pineapple juice
2 tbsp cider vinegar
1 egg

3 bananas, mashed
1 cup crushed pineapple, drained
1 cup diced pears
12 maraschino cherries

1 cup heavy cream, whipped

COOK – Cook first 6 ingredients until thick.

ADD – Add next 4 ingredients.

FOLD IN – Fold in whipped cream. Pour into 8-9" square pan.

FREEZE – Freeze. Cut into squares to serve.

A traditional addition to
luncheons in the South!

Sylvia Johnson
Partner

111

CREAM OF BROCCOLI SOUP

⅓ cup each: leek, onion, & celery, diced
1 cup broccoli, diced
3 tbsp butter
½ cup white wine

3 tbsp flour
3 cups chicken stock

salt, pepper, and thyme to taste

1 cup light cream

SAUTÉ – Sauté vegetables in butter and wine for 5 minutes on low.

THICKEN – Blend in flour, then chicken stock. Bring to a boil.

SIMMER – Season. Let simmer until vegetables are tender. Add cream.

MAKES – 4½ cups

Elegant! Serve with French bread, a simple salad, and a glass of wine.

Alice Berg – Partner

SUPERß FRENCH DRESSING

½ cup vinegar (herb
     flavored is nice)
¾ cup salad or olive
     oil (or a mixture)
1 cup catsup
¼ cup sugar
1 small onion, finely
     chopped
1 tsp salt
½ tsp celery seed
¼ tsp paprika

MIX – Combine all ingredients and beat with mixer or blender for about 30 seconds.

TOSS – Toss with favorite salad ingredients.

Whenever there is a get-together,
I make the salad!

Mary Ellen Von Holt – Partner

BROCCOLI PARMESAN

20 oz frozen
  broccoli
2 eggs, slightly
  beaten
14½-oz can stewed
  tomatoes

10¾-oz can
  cheddar cheese
  soup

Parmesan cheese,
  grated
oregano

PREPARE – Cook and drain broccoli. Place in a buttered casserole. Pour eggs over broccoli. Add tomatoes and cheese soup. Top with grated Parmesan and oregano.

BAKE – Bake, uncovered, at 350° for 30 minutes.

What could be easier?

Joan Korth
Staff

SCALLOPED POTATOES WITH CHEESE

32 oz frozen hash browns, thawed
16 oz sour cream
8 oz mild cheese, grated
2 10¾-oz cans cream of potato soup
¼ cup onions, chopped
2 tsp salt

Parmesan cheese, grated

MIX – Mix first 6 ingredients. Pour into 9x13" baking pan. Sprinkle Parmesan on top.

BAKE – Bake covered at 350° for 1 hour or uncovered at 325° for 25-30 minutes.

Delicious and oh-so-simple to prepare!

Pat Myers
Staff

MEDITERRANEAN RICE SALAD

1 cup rice, uncooked

1 red bell pepper, chopped

1 green bell pepper, chopped

1 cup slivered almonds

chopped fresh parsley, lots

1 cup green olives, sliced

1 cup raisins

3 tbsp olive oil

7 tbsp wine vinegar

COOK – Cook rice and cool.

MIX – Mix all ingredients. Chill.

A family favorite with no leftovers!

Jennifer Suter
Staff

SEAFOOD PASTA PRIMAVERA

½ lb jumbo shrimp, cleaned & deveined
¼ lb sea scallops
½ lb fresh broccoli flowerets
¼ cup dried tomatoes
1 cup julienne carrots
4 cloves garlic, minced
¼ cup olive oil

½ cup garbanzo beans
1 tbsp pine nuts
¼ tsp red pepper flakes
½ cup chicken broth
½ cup Parmesan, grated
½ lb angel hair pasta, cooked

SAUTÉ – Sauté seafood and vegetables in olive oil until shrimp is pink.

ADD – Add garbanzos, pine nuts, red pepper, and chicken broth. Simmer 10 minutes.

TOSS – Toss with the cheese. Serve over pasta.

Impressive!

Marianne Webb
Staff

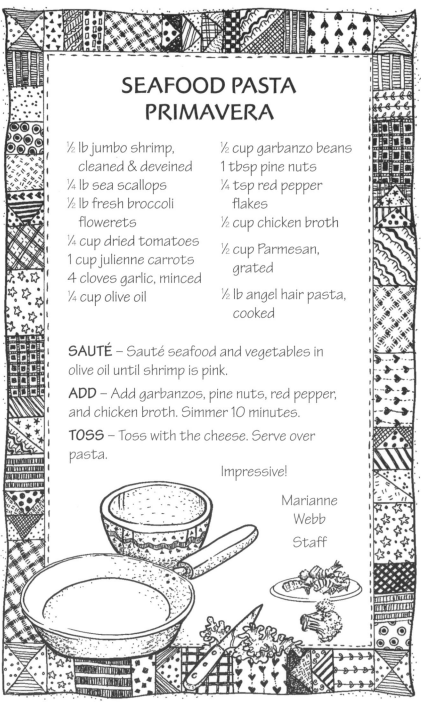

117

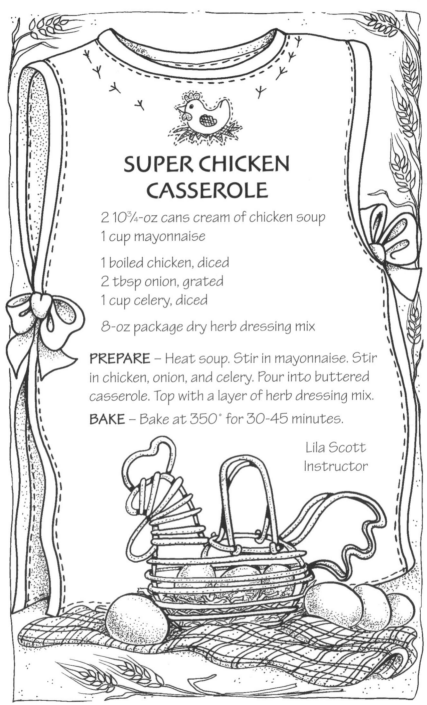

SUPER CHICKEN CASSEROLE

2 10¾-oz cans cream of chicken soup
1 cup mayonnaise

1 boiled chicken, diced
2 tbsp onion, grated
1 cup celery, diced

8-oz package dry herb dressing mix

PREPARE – Heat soup. Stir in mayonnaise. Stir in chicken, onion, and celery. Pour into buttered casserole. Top with a layer of herb dressing mix.

BAKE – Bake at 350° for 30-45 minutes.

Lila Scott
Instructor

EASY PORKCHOP CASSEROLE

½ cup onion, chopped
½ cup celery, chopped
¼ cup slivered almonds
butter or margarine
7-oz can mushrooms,
   drained

salt & pepper to taste

4 large, lean, boneless
   porkchops, trimmed

1 egg, beaten
1 cup dried bread crumbs
cooking oil

6 tbsp long-grain rice,
   uncooked
10½-oz can beef broth

sliced apple or tomato
   (optional)

SAUTÉ – Sauté first 3 ingredients in butter or margarine until onion and celery are tender-crisp. Add mushrooms. Season with salt and pepper.

BROWN – Dip chops in egg, then in crumbs. Brown in small amount of oil and drain on paper towels.

LAYER – Place rice in 8 x 8″ baking pan or casserole. Top with vegetable mixture. Pour broth over all. Place chops on top. Place apple or tomato slice on each chop, if desired. Seal with foil.

BAKE – Bake at 350° for 1½ hours.

Pop this in the oven and go back to your quilting!

Anne Anderberg – Instructor

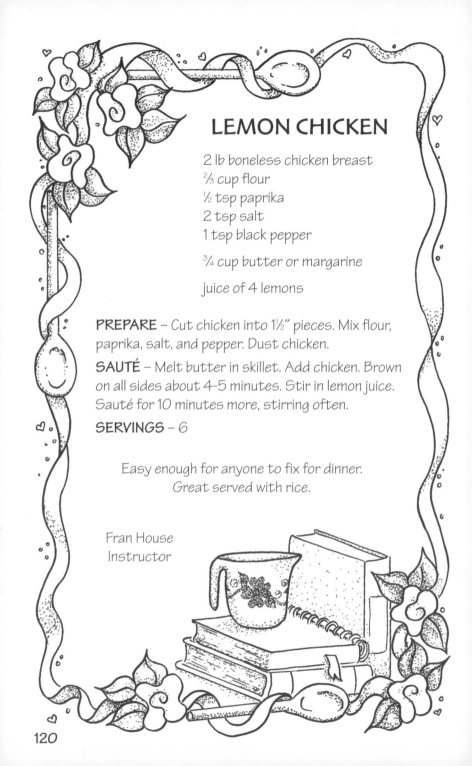

LEMON CHICKEN

2 lb boneless chicken breast
⅔ cup flour
½ tsp paprika
2 tsp salt
1 tsp black pepper

¾ cup butter or margarine

juice of 4 lemons

PREPARE – Cut chicken into 1½" pieces. Mix flour, paprika, salt, and pepper. Dust chicken.

SAUTÉ – Melt butter in skillet. Add chicken. Brown on all sides about 4-5 minutes. Stir in lemon juice. Sauté for 10 minutes more, stirring often.

SERVINGS – 6

Easy enough for anyone to fix for dinner.
Great served with rice.

Fran House
Instructor

LEMON-LIME
SODA CAKE

1½ cups butter   1 tbsp vanilla
3 cups sugar   ¾ cup lemon-
5 eggs   lime soda
3 cups flour

MIX – Butter and flour a large bundt pan.
Cream butter and sugar until light and
fluffy. Add eggs 1 at a time. Add flour, then
vanilla. Fold in soda. Pour into prepared pan.

BAKE – Bake at 325° for 75 minutes or
until done.

A surprise ingredient—
wonderful cake!

Tina Schuman
Staff

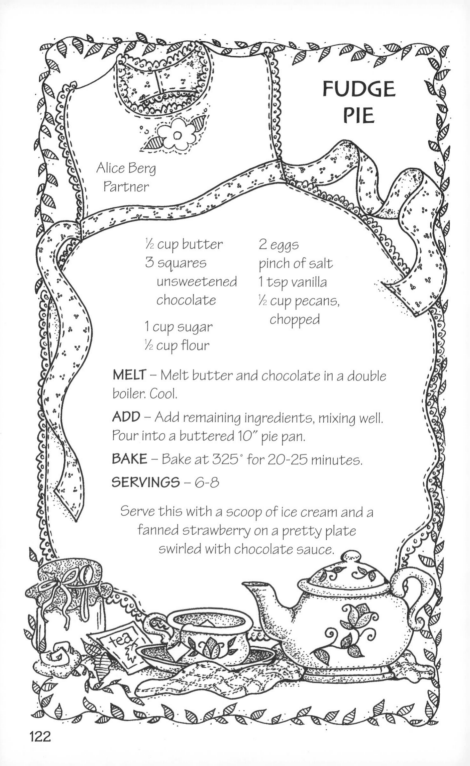

FUDGE PIE

Alice Berg
Partner

½ cup butter
3 squares
   unsweetened
   chocolate

1 cup sugar
½ cup flour

2 eggs
pinch of salt
1 tsp vanilla
½ cup pecans,
   chopped

MELT – Melt butter and chocolate in a double boiler. Cool.

ADD – Add remaining ingredients, mixing well. Pour into a buttered 10" pie pan.

BAKE – Bake at 325° for 20-25 minutes.

SERVINGS – 6-8

Serve this with a scoop of ice cream and a fanned strawberry on a pretty plate swirled with chocolate sauce.

CREAM CHEESE SQUARES

⅓ cup butter
⅓ cup brown sugar
1 cup flour
½ cup nuts, chopped

¼ cup sugar
1 tbsp lemon juice

8 oz cream cheese, softened
1 egg, beaten
2 tbsp milk
½ tsp vanilla

MIX – Cream butter and sugar. Stir in flour then nuts. Reserve some for topping. Pack remainder firmly into an 8 x 8" square pan.

BAKE – Bake at 350° for 10 minutes.

MIX – Blend sugar, lemon juice and cream cheese. Add egg, milk and vanilla. Pour over the baked crust. Crumble remaining flour mixture over top.

BAKE – Bake at 350° for 25 minutes. Cool. Cut into squares. Refrigerate.

Alice Berg
Partner

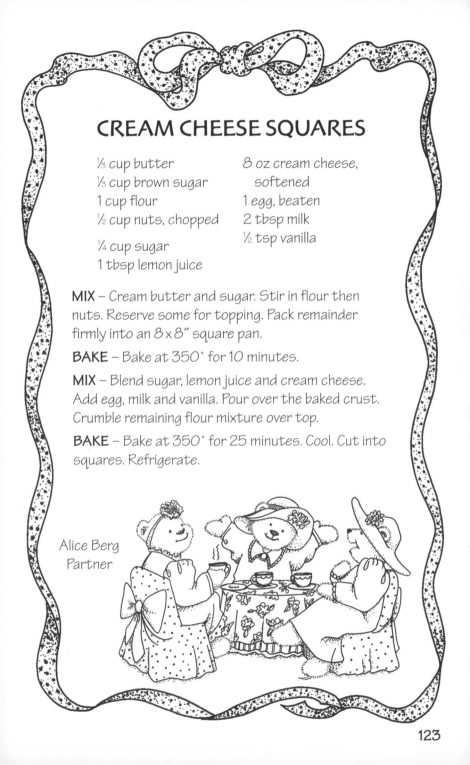

QUILTING HINTS

When quilting for long periods at a time, place a piece of red cloth, any other red object, at a distance. Look up at it occasionally and rest your eyes. Doing this refocuses the eyes and helps to relieve eyestrain.

Applique Tips: To help prevent fraying, use a moistened toothpick to help turn under the edges of the applique. Another way to control frayed threads is to use a dab of glue from a fabric glue stick on the tip of the needle.

To keep bias binding from tangling and stretching when attaching it to a bed-size quilt, roll the binding and put it in a ziplock baggie. Close the baggie except for about one inch in the corner. The binding will stay neat and roll out easily as you sew it to the quilt.

To eliminate clutter on sewing and cutting surfaces, hang wire shelf storage units from edge of table for storing rulers, scissors, and other tools.

Store templates in a plastic page protector labeled with the project name. Keep page protectors in a three-ring binder.

Project
Pages

Photocopy the recipe card below on cardstock.
Color patchwork with permanent markers, if desired.

RECIPE FOR: _____

FROM THE KITCHEN OF: _____

TEA COZY

Fits pots 5" high by up to 22" around

BUY

⅜ yd. main fabric (42" wide)
⅜ yd. lining
⅜ yd. batting
1¼ yds. ⅜" wide ribbon
⅓ yd. ¼" elastic

CUT

main fabric – two pieces 10½ x 14½"
lining – two pieces 10½ x 14½"
batting – four pieces 7 x 13½"

See page 127 for drawing of finished project.

1. Make two "sides" with the four fabric pieces. Layer one lining piece and one main fabric piece right sides together. Using a ¼" seam allowance, stitch three sides, leaving the 14½" bottom open. Clip corners. Turn right side out and press. Repeat with other main fabric and lining pieces.

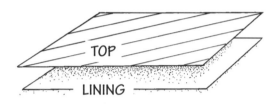

2. Press under ¼" hem on unfinished edges of both "sides".

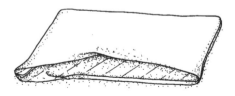

3. On both "sides", draw two lines from top finished edge, one 1½" down and one 2" down. Stitch along both lines to form ribbon casing.

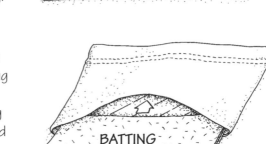

4. Lay two pieces of batting between top and lining with top edge of batting next to stitched casing. Pin batting to hold in place and pin bottom opening closed. Repeat with other "side".

BATTING

5. On both "sides", stitch across bottom as close to edge as possible. Make one more line of stitching ½" up from first stitching to form casing for elastic. Do not catch batting in stitching. With seam ripper, clip the few stitches at the beginning and end of each casing line.

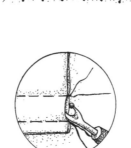

6. Thread elastic through bottom casing of one piece and continue through other casing on second piece. Thread the ribbon through the top casing of both pieces. Adjust the elastic to fit your pot and stitch ends securely. Pull on ribbon and tie to fit pot.

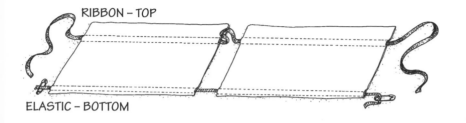

RIBBON – TOP

ELASTIC – BOTTOM

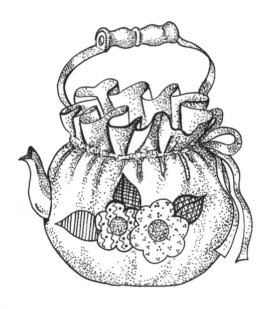

Optional: Add this floral applique, page 128, or the heart applique, page 129, after Step 5.

 BREAD CLOTH

BUY
1⅜ yds. fabric (42″ wide)
scraps for appliques
⅝ yd. thin cotton batting

CUT
fabric – two 18½″ squares
two 2½×42″ strips
batting – one 18½″ square

1. Applique flowers and leaves in one corner or all four corners of one of the 18½″ squares of fabric using your favorite method.

2. Lightly mark a crosshatch pattern on the appliqued square with a pencil. Layer unappliqued square (right side down), then batting, then appliqued square (right side up). Baste.

3. Quilt by hand or machine.

4. Stitch strips together end to end. Press in half lengthwise, wrong sides together. Bind edge of bread cloth, mitering corners.

PAPIER-MÂCHÉ BOXES

BUY
papier-mâché box
fabric scraps for appliques
fusible web

1. Following fusible web manufacturer's directions, bond fabric appliques to papier-mâché box. Use one of the patterns on pages 128-129.

2. If desired, add penstitched details with permanent markers.

3. If desired, paint box with a water-based varnish using a sponge brush. Apply several light coats. Test varnish first on chosen fabrics.

   Note: Fusible web applique with fabric works great on paper bags as well.

Use for cookies, cracker snack mix, muffins, and more.

CASSEROLE CARRIER

Fits 9x13" baking dish

BUY	CUT
1½ yds fabric (42" wide)	fabric – 2 pieces 10½ x 41½"
¾ yd. of batting	2 pieces 14½ x 32½"
2 wooden spoons, 18" long	batting – 1 piece 10½ x 41½"
¼ yd. Velcro® strips	1 piece 14½ x 32½"

See page 132 for drawing of finished project.

1. Inside Flap: Lay the two 10½ x 41½" fabric pieces right sides together on top of the batting.

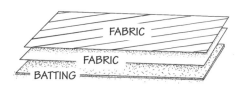

Using a ¼" seam allowance, stitch around all four sides, leaving an opening for turning. Clip corners, turn right side out, and press. Whipstitch opening closed.

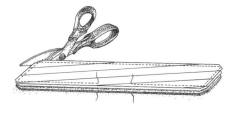

Mark quilting lines every 2". Machine quilt along drawn lines.

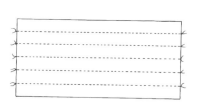

2. Outside Flap: Lay the remaining two fabric pieces right sides together on top of the batting. Repeat above directions for stitching and quilting.

3. Make a template of the handle-opening guide on page 132. Lay guide along center of each end of outside flap. Mark with a pencil and then cut opening. Turn under ¼" hem along handle opening, clipping as needed. Topstitch close to fold and again ¼" away. Repeat at other end. Optional Bind with purchased bias tape

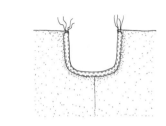

4. Fold 2" of the straight edge at either side of the curved opening to inside to form casings. Slipstitch in place. Repeat on other side.

5. Lay inside flap along center of wrong side of outside flap at right angles. Stitch around the rectangle formed by the crossover. Double stitch for strength.

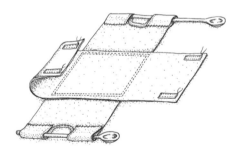

6. Cut two pieces of Velcro® each 4½" long. Stitch to corners of inside flap as shown. Insert two wooden spoons into the casings for the handles.

TOP EDGE OF FLAP

HANDLE-OPENING GUIDE

HANDLE OPENING

CENTER OF FLAP – Place on Center Fold

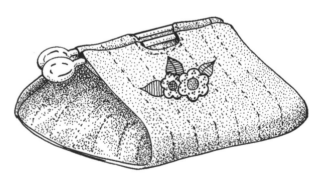

Optional: Add this floral applique, page 128, or
the heart applique, page 129, after Step 4.

PLACE MATS

14½"x18½"

BUY – *Makes 4*
1 yd. main fabric (42" wide)
1 yd. backing
1 yd. thin batting or
   needlepunch

CUT
main fabric – four pieces 14½"x18½"
backing – four pieces 15½"x19½"
batting – cut four pieces 15½"x19½"

If desired, applique main fabric rectangle with one of the patterns on pages 128-129 before making place mat.

1. Layer batting, backing (right side up), and main fabric (right side down and centered). Main fabric will be slightly smaller than batting and backing.

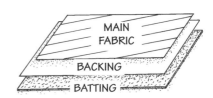

2. With batting on bottom and using a ¼" seam allowance, stitch around entire place mat, leaving an opening along one edge for turning. Trim batting and backing to fit place mat. Clip corners.

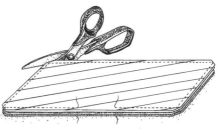

3. Turn right side out, press, and slipstitch opening closed.

4. Topstitch around place mat, ½" from edges.

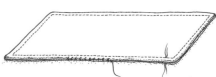

COOKIE BAG

12½x5½x4"

BUY
½ yd. main fabric (42" wide)
½ yd. lining fabric (42" wide)
⅝ yd. paper-backed fusible web
6" square clear vinyl .4 mil thick

CUT
main fabric – 15x19½" rectangle
lining fabric – 15x19½" rectangle
fusible web – 15x19½" rectangle

See page 136 for drawing of finished project.

1. Lay fusible web on wrong side of main fabric rectangle. Fuse, following manufacturer's directions. Peel off paper backing and fuse main fabric rectangle to lining rectangle, wrong sides together. Fold rectangle in half, crosswise, and lightly crease to mark center front.

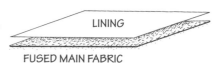

LINING

FUSED MAIN FABRIC

CENTER FRONT

2. Window
   Pattern on page 136

   a. Make a template of heart shape. Using template, draw shape on lining side of fused fabric along center front line 6½" down from top edge of bag.

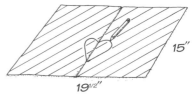

15"

19½"

   b. Stitch on marked line with matching thread. Mark a line ¼" to the inside of the stitched line. Cut fabric on line. Clip all curves and diagonally into corners.

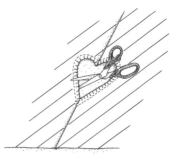

c. Press ¼" to lining side
   so stitching line does
   not show on front of
   bag.

d. Place vinyl square over
   opening on lining side of
   fused fabric and pin in
   place.

e. On main fabric side,
   topstitch close to edge
   of heart shape. Trim
   vinyl.

3. Fold bag in half, main fabric
   sides together. Stitch
   center back seam with a
   ¼" seam allowance.

4. Fold bag so center seam is
   aligned with center front.
   Stitch across bottom of
   bag with a ¼" seam
   allowance.

5. For boxed bottom, refold on
   corner at bottom of bag to
   match diagram. Measure 2"
   from corner and draw a line
   perpendicular to seam.
   Stitch on line. Repeat at
   other corner.

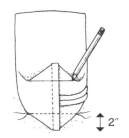

2"

Turn bag right side out.

6. Press a ¼" hem to inside of bag at top edge. Topstitch very close to cut edge. Press sides of bag, measuring in 2".

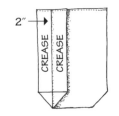

CASSEROLE CADDY

For 8" square casserole dish

BUY

1⅛ yds. cotton fabric (42" wide)
⅝ yd. thin cotton batting
heavy cardboard

Prewash fabric and batting so caddy will fit after subsequent launderings.

See page 139 for drawing of finished project.

CUT FABRIC

base – 14" square
         15" square
pocket – 9x9½" rectangle
pockets – four 6x9" rectangles
ties – eight 1½x12" rectangles

CUT BATTING

15" square

CUT CARDBOARD

7¼" square
four 2x7¼" squares

1. Layer in order and pin well:
   a. batting square
   b. large fabric square, right side up
   c. small fabric square, right side down, centered on others

2. Stitch around small square with a ⅜" seam allowance, leaving 4" open on one side for turning. Trim large squares even with small square. Clip corners. Turn through opening so batting is sandwiched between fabric layers. Press. Pin opening closed. Topstitch very close to entire outside edge of caddy.

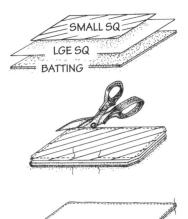

3. Lightly mark a diagonal 2" grid on outside of caddy and machine quilt on the lines.

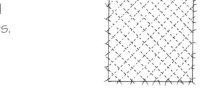

4. Mark fold lines on inside of caddy, as shown, 2½" from each side.

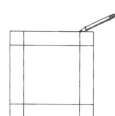

5. Hem one 9" side of center pocket piece: press ½" to wrong side, then press ½" to wrong side again. Stitch close to fold. Pocket should measure 8½" high by 9" wide.

½"
½"

8½"
9"

6. Lay pocket wrong side down on inside of caddy, matching hemmed edge with one marked fold line. Tuck under and pin the three raw edges to meet marked fold lines on caddy. Press pocket. Stitch pinned edges very close to folds.

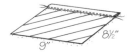

7. Press the 1½ x12" pieces for ties in half lengthwise, wrong sides together. Unfold. Press long raw edges in to meet pressed line. See diagram. Fold in one end, then refold along center line. Stitch across end and along double-folded edge.

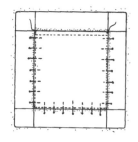

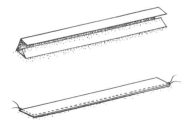

8. Press the four 6x9" pieces for the side pockets in half lengthwise, wrong sides together. Pieces should measure 3x9". Lay one side pocket on side of caddy with fold next to edge of center pocket. See diagram. Tuck under and pin the three raw edges to meet marked fold lines and outside edge of caddy. Press pocket. Repeat for other three side pockets.

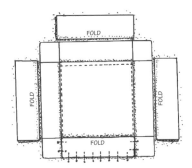

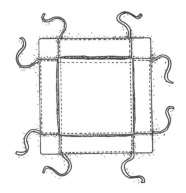

9. Tuck raw end of a tie under corner of side pocket at each corner as shown. Pin in place. Stitch pinned edges of pockets, catching ties in stitching.

10. Trim cardboard pieces slightly, if necessary, to fit pockets. Slide cardboard pieces into pockets. Fold side up and tie each corner in a bow.

Optional: Add applique to center pocket after Step 5. Pattern on page 128.

CALICO BEAN SOUP MIX

For 16 great gifts or bazaar items, combine beans, divide into 16 no-sew bags, and attach the soup recipe below.

1 lb each, dried:
black beans
pinto beans
red beans
kidney beans
navy beans
Great Northern beans
baby lima beans

large lima beans
green split peas
yellow split peas
black-eyed peas
red lentils
green lentils
brown lentils

  ## CALICO BEAN SOUP

2 cups Calico Bean
Soup Mix

1 smoked ham hock
1 medium onion, chopped
2 ribs celery, chopped
1 clove garlic, minced
1 bay leaf
6 cups water

2 14½-oz cans stewed
  tomatoes
¼ cup chopped fresh
  parsley
1 tbsp red wine vinegar
2 tsp salt

1 tsp each pepper, chili
  powder, & cumin

SOAK – Wash and sort beans. Cover with water and soak overnight. Drain. Place in stockpot.
SIMMER – Add next 6 ingredients. Bring to a boil, reduce heat to medium-low. Cover. Simmer 1 hour, adding water if needed.
ADD – Add remaining ingredients. Simmer 1 hour or until beans are tender.
SERVINGS – 6-8

NO-SEW BAG FOR CALICO BEAN SOUP MIX

$6\frac{1}{2} \times 9\frac{1}{2}''$

BUY – Makes 2
¼ yd. main fabric (42" wide)
¼"-wide paper-backed fusible
   web tape
raffia or twine

CUT
fabric – $7\frac{1}{2} \times 20''$ rectangle

1. Press fabric rectangle in half crosswise, right sides together. Unfold. Following manufacturer's directions, fuse web tape on right side of fabric along sides, ending at center fold. Remove paper backing. Refold fabric and fuse.

2. Hem: Fuse web tape along top edge on wrong side of bag. Press ½" hem to wrong side. Unfold edge and remove paper backing. Refold edge and fuse hem in place.

4. Turn bag right side out. Push corners out carefully. Press, making sure seam allowances lie flat.

5. Place 2 cups soup mix in bag. Tie several lengths of raffia or twine into a bow around top of bag. Attach soup recipe.

141

RECIPE INDEX

MAIN DISHES

DESSERTS

PROJECT INDEX